Telling
Stories
the Kiowa Way

Telling
Stories
the Kiowa Way

GUS PALMER JR.

The University of Arizona Press   Tucson

The University of Arizona Press

www.uapress.arizona.edu

Library of Congress Cataloging-in-Publication Data
Palmer, Gus, 1943–
Telling stories the Kiowa way / Gus Palmer, Jr.
p. cm.
Includes bibliographical references and index.
ISBN 0-8165-2277-4 (cloth : alk. paper) —
ISBN 0-8165-2278-2 (pbk. : alk. paper)
1. Kiowa Indians—Folklore.   2. Storytelling—Great Plains.
3. Tales—Great Plains.   I. Title.
E99.K5 P35 2003
398'.089'9749—dc21
2002013895

Manufactured in the United States of America on acid-free,
archival-quality paper containing a minimum of 30% post-consumer
waste and processed chlorine free.

1 3 1 2 1 1 1 0 0 9 0 8 7 6 5 4 3 2

for Carolyn

Contents

Acknowledgments

I wish to acknowledge the help and kindness of my Kiowa storytelling consultants John Tofpi, Cornelius Spottedhorse, my parents, Gus and Alice Palmer, Dorothy Kodaseet, Carole Willis, my *thê* (uncles) the late Oscar Tsoodle and the late Parker P. McKenzie, and my *kọ́:gí* (grandfather) the late Henry Tenadooah. I also wish to acknowledge the support and assistance of the Kiowa Nation of Oklahoma and the Department of Anthropology at the University of Oklahoma. For their generous assistance, thoughtful advice, and encouragement, I am especially indebted to Professors Margaret Bender, Loretta Fowler, John Dunn, Alan Velie, Circe Sturm, Jason Jackson, and Morris Foster. Finally, I want to thank Yvonne Reineke and Nancy Arora at the University of Arizona Press.

Introduction

All right, this is how we tell stories.
It ain't much but that's all we got.

Two things help John Tofpi get through his daily life. They are his tribal beliefs and storytelling. Around eighty-two years old, this gregarious Kiowa is a fairly able-bodied man for his age. He likes to talk and joke a lot, but what he likes doing most, everybody around Carnegie, Oklahoma, knows, is tell funny stories. Likable and always having interesting things to say, he is, I found, agreeable, sensitive, and very often wise as a storytelling consultant. When I told my mother I was consulting with him on contemporary storytelling, she narrowed her eyes in the way she used to do when I was a boy and did or said something so foolish or stupid she couldn't believe it.

"Oh me," she laughed. "He's not a storyteller, is he?" She was standing over the stove stirring a pot of boiling meat. It was sunny outdoors. Shafts of sunlight poured in the window. It had been hot all week, and I had almost changed my mind about coming down to visit.

"Here," my mother said, clearing things off the table. "Sit right down and taste this."

The meat smelled good, and I couldn't wait to try some. I hadn't eaten any of her cooking in a long time. She removed the pot from the stove and set it on the table.

"That John Sáuibé [Slow]. Can you find anybody else? There must be a thousand Kiowas who tell stories."

"You don't have to know lots of things, Mom. Just Kiowa stories. It's like this soup. Some people like fat in theirs. They cut up the meat and leave a lot of fat on it for flavor. They put in potatoes. They mix in onions. They boil the meat just like grandma used to do until it's so tender it falls off the bone. People tell stories just like people make boiled meat, Mom. All kinds of ways."

John Tofpi and I are related. He is about as old as my mother. In the Kiowa way, we are supposed to be brothers. The Kiowa way is simply how Kiowa people relate tribally to things, each other, and the world. For example, there is no Kiowa word for cousin. For Kiowas, the concept of cousin is essentially nonexistent, so you refer to all of your male cousins as your brothers and all your female cousins as your sisters. I have heard John T. address my mother as Mom just the way I do. The first time I heard him call her Momma I snickered.

"Does he know anything?"

Peanut, my mother's pet chihuahua, skittered between my feet under the table.

"Come here, fool." I reached down and touched the small dog on the top of the head. "*Hàu*," I said, raising up. "He knows more things than most Kiowas. Besides," I said, using his Kiowa name, "Sáuibé is easy to talk to, Mom. And he has interesting things to say, too. Do you think you can fatten up this Peanut enough to tender roast?"

"Peanut's a she. She's my friend."

"Who, Peanut? She'd make a good steak sandwich. When I look at you, I see a well-baked roast sitting in a roasting pan," I told my mother's small dog. "You remind of one of those prairie dogs Séndé knocked in the head that time on the prairie plains and roasted so tender the meat fell off its bones. Do you know that, fool? You remember that story, Mom?"

"How could I forget."

Séndé is the Kiowa trickster hero in traditional stories. The equivalent of Wile E. Coyote, Séndé is clever, outrageous, and mean. In one tale he tricks a bunch of prairie dogs into dancing with their eyes shut tightly and then proceeds to knock them in the head until he has enough slain to roast on an open fire he has already prepared.

Introduction

"It's the way he tells stories, Mom. You know, Kiowa ones."

My mother's face brightened with a smile. "Is it?"

"You know, Mom, Sáuibé knows just about everybody in town. Every Kiowa alive knows Sáuibé and he knows them. He's full of news all the time and is funny at that. I mean telling jokes and things."

"Well, that's good then."

"You should hear him, Mom. He's not afraid to say anything."

I knew I had found the person I was looking for. I didn't want any celebrity Kiowa. I wanted a simple, everyday, run-of-the-mill Kiowa person. I'd promised myself before I came out to do fieldwork with the Kiowas that I would stick to my plan, which was to work with people I thought would sit down with me and tell stories and talk about storytelling in great detail. I thought I knew some Kiowas who could do that. John Tofpi was a good choice. He was straightforward and honest. He was not only a relative of mine. He was also somebody who knew lots of stories and people. I knew I could count on him to tell things just as they are. Besides, he had an engaging way of saying things.

"It'll be perfect," I explained to my mother. "He's exactly the kind of consultant I need. He doesn't claim that he knows everything like some Kiowas do. You know how they are around here. I'm not looking for an expert, because the kind of fieldwork I'm doing has to do with plain Kiowas telling stories. Storytelling isn't such a specialized undertaking for Kiowas, you know."

My mother looked at me a moment and then smiled. Peanut did the same.

"Everybody tells stories, Beeshee. Kiowas I mean. Your grandpa knew lots of stories. He could tell you everything you need to know."

"Mom, John Sáuibé is the best choice. Besides, he has time to talk about all those good Kiowa things I care so much about."

I was feeling accomplished, and I explained what I was doing and how I was going to do it. Kiowas like to know the details. I broke off a piece of fry bread and dipped it into the pot of boiled meat my mother had set in front of me.

I think I have heard or known some of the best old Kiowa stories, the so-called stuff of tribal origins and myths. These were, it seems, sealed in my soul forever. Many of the Kiowa values I learned as a boy, I believe, came directly out of these narratives. But like many young Kiowas, I had drifted away from the teachings. That is, they seemed suddenly irrelevant. I found myself wanting to find out for myself what there was in the world outside the confines of Kiowa culture. In order to do this I had to change how I thought about things in my life because, somehow in my youthful mind, the old ways interfered with what was actually going on and new around me. I wanted to get out and see the world. And so I did. When I was about fifteen I went to find work in the next town.

Anadarko, Oklahoma, was an exciting place. There were interesting people to meet. Some of the best Kiowa artists lived in that Indian agency town. The local post office featured life-sized murals painted on its walls. There were scenes of dancers, buffalo chases, and encampments. One mural showed two Indian boys, wrestling, encircled by about a half dozen other boys. The artist had captured the look of youthful determination and energy of the pair. And I doubt that I shall ever forget that mural, because I too was young and determined to experience and accomplish wonderful things in the world.

I found work at a small outdoor tourist facility outside Anadarko. I was hired to dance and entertain the tourists. Dancing and meeting and talking to so many people made a huge impression on me. That summer was my first exposure to the world at large. It was exciting and fun. For the first time in my life I was free to move about and do things I had only dreamed of. It did not occur to me then that I should ever return to the place of my birth, not for any reason. But I did, many years later: to live and work among my people. And that is when I saw what it was to be a Kiowa in the full sense of that reality.

Now, at my feet, Peanut yipped merrily and jumped up and down like a tiny windup toy.

"You need to fatten up this critter of yours, Mom," I said, chewing and swallowing the tender meat. "You still have it in the cooking department, don't you?"

"Here, use this spoon. It's bigger." My mother handed me a larger spoon. "There's a bowl if you want it." She pointed with her lips toward her side table. I loved seeing my mother gesture like that. It made me feel right at home.

"Sáuibé's Oma's brother," continued my mother.

"I know it."

Oma was one of my mother's favorite relatives. They grew up together. They were close. They ran around just as I did with my cousins. I remember Oma well. She had more children than any Kiowa woman I knew. I went to school with her boys at Carnegie. One of them, Jay, was one of my closest friends.

"Ramona and Matthew too."

"There were a bunch in his family, Mom."

"Oh yes."

We used to call Jay Chicken. Ironically, he was one of the most fearless persons in the world. He'd take on a bear if he had to. I envied him for his brave heart and wished I was as tough as he was. He had a so-called classical Indian nose. It made him stand out among the other boys like a movie star Indian.

My mother patted me on the knee. "I'm glad you got your brother to help you."

I thought about the time John Tofpi told me about Sam Martin, my mother's only brother, who died when he was about ten years old. John told me they were real close. They lived only a few miles apart. Sam Martin died of a rare disease.

My mother cared a lot for John Tofpi, just as she did all of her Kiowa relatives. Kiowas have a great capacity for close family ties. Kiowas are bonded more closely than any people I know. Almost every Kiowa is related to another Kiowa in one way or another, whether as a cousin, a grandpa, a grandma, an uncle, or an aunt. I have cousins I don't even know until I go to the Fourth of July powwow down at Carnegie Park where a stranger might materialize out of the clear blue as mysteriously as Captain Kirk or Spock, extend a hand, and tell me proudly that he is a long-lost relative. Sometimes my mother would lead an old, old woman up by the hand and introduce me to her: "Here, sonny, this is your grandma on our side of the family. Now shake her hand. Next time you see her be sure to acknowledge her in the old Kiowa way."

It's really very awkward sometimes and embarrassing, because you want to acknowledge the relationship but don't know how to do it. When I was a young man trying to date a Kiowa girl, it was awful because I didn't know whether or not I was kin to the girl I'd taken a fancy to. To keep from being disappointed I'd wait a few days before telling my mother about a female acquaintance. And then of course she'd drill me in a kind of offhanded way, as if it was just about the most natural thing in the world to do.

"Who is she?" my mother would start out.

"Um, her name is Katy, Mom."

"Oh? Katy who?"

"Oh, Katy something. I don't remember."

"You don't remember? She must have a last name. Who are her parents?"

"Her parents? Joe—no, it's Bill and, I don't know, Guoladdle."

"Guoladdle? Oh, no, no. Oh, dear me, she's your cousin! You're related to her on your grandpa's side! You can't do that! It's out of the question!"

Yes. It was tough trying to meet a Kiowa girl back home when I was a young man. But that was how it was, which is another subject, but it helps to clarify this whole business of Kiowa kinship right here. That Kiowas put a lot of stock in how they are related to other Kiowas is pretty well known in southwestern Oklahoma. As it turns out, Kiowas are actually one big family in ways that puzzle most non-Indians. They can't believe you have so many grandpas and uncles and brothers. And this is what my mother was trying to point out to me when I mentioned that I was working with John Tofpi as my story consultant. John T., or Sáuibé, is my mother's cousin on her father's side, something I more or less knew. Being related as I was meant easy access to stories. I honestly needed a good and reliable consultant and couldn't think of anybody else when I first arrived at the Kiowa Elders Center some time back to locate someone. Kiowas don't usually like to tell intimate details to strangers. Kiowas prefer to keep stories within a relatively tight, informal

Introduction

circle of close friends and relatives. I knew this, and so it was easy for me to approach John T. as well as the other story consultants with whom I worked. Besides, as I was saying, John T. had other good qualities as a consultant: he knows just about everybody in Kiowa country. White and Indian. He has his finger on the pulse of Kiowa Indian country, and all of this makes for a perfect storytelling coworker.

After I pointed out some of John T.'s other good qualities, my mother agreed that Sáuibé was the best choice. Peanut was suddenly under the table again, looking up at me and showing her tiny sharp teeth in a grin.

"Are you pleased with my choice or because I came down for a visit, doggie?" I wondered if Peanut understood the Kiowa language the way the old Kiowa dogs used to. My grandfather used to tell me stories about Kiowas and dogs.

"You hungry, little fool?" I reached down and tried to touch Peanut on the head, but she hurtled like a missile into the next room.

"He's your relative. You need to call him *fàbí* (brother)."

"Hàu. I know it," I said, thinking these new arrangements I was making meant that I might have to do something special in recognition. Kiowas like ceremony. A good friend of mine reminded me of this fact when he happened to walk up when an uncle of mine and I were discussing the difference between his people, the Choctaws, and us Kiowas.

"You know the Kiowas are different than my people," said my Choctaw friend. "You know why? Because they like ceremony. Ceremonial things."

Yes, I think I had responded. My uncle and I had been discussing our own Choctaw background, which is minuscule but important to us all the same. We were bemoaning the fact that we never learned any Choctaw culture—or language, for that matter, not a single word—when my friend had strolled up.

"Our people don't have that anymore," explained my Choctaw friend. "Kiowas, on the other hand, do those ceremonial things all the time. That's good."

I was a little confused at the time because I didn't know right away what he was getting at, and so I asked him.

"Well, friend, take for instance, dance. Kiowas still do their traditional dances. They sing the old songs, my friend. You don't find too much of that with lots of tribes around here."

He spoke with real authority, and I had to concur with what he said. If you record something Kiowa, say a story or song, you might have to pay for it or do something special in recognition of the transaction. You reciprocate. It shows respect, appreciation. For Kiowas, there is this kind of rule of thumb: when you give somebody something you supposedly own, say a song, that person has to make a return gift of some kind. Most traditional Kiowas can be very formalistic about things like song give-aways. You have to be careful if you decide to sing a song that somebody else owns. You can't sing it unless you ask special permission from the owner of that song. This custom can be tedious for outsiders. There is often a lot of misunderstanding between Kiowas and other people for this very reason. Say a person, a non-Kiowa, asks a Kiowa to record a song. Now this can be a personal song, or, say, an Óhòmàu, sacred dance society, composition owned by somebody the Kiowa knows or to whom he or she is related. In order to do this, the non-Kiowa must make some outward sign or gesture in recognition of the gift. Or better, must show, preferably publicly, that something important has been exchanged between two people. Money, a blanket, or some sort of gift exchange must take place. It is not the payment that is so important here as it is the recognition of something significant happening: the exchange, the song going from one party to another. That is what is important and why it *is* ceremonial. You, as a Kiowa, must acknowledge in some special way the occasion of the gift giving or the gift itself. It is like the exchange of gifts between two persons who care about each other very much. Give-aways at powwows are a good example here. When Indians make a give-away at a powwow, they are by and large not only extending the life of the shawl they might be giving to a relation or, in some instances, to a stranger. They also are extending the life or ceremony of the giving itself. It marks an existential moment of giving, so to speak. It is the hallmark of well-being, Kiowaness, tribalism.[1]

When one receives a gift at a powwow give-away, that item, whatever it is, is not generally kept. The difference here is that most non-Indians would be offended if you gave away a gift they gave you. Not most tradi-

Introduction

tional Kiowas or traditional Indians. A Kiowa gift, if given in the traditional sense, needs be passed on to somebody else just as it was received, ritually. The closest thing to give-away, Indian style, is the kind of exchange Bronislaw Malinowski (1922) observed going on among the Trobriand people in the South Seas. Here, he observed, the people exchange *kula* in a ceremonial way that maintains a network of mutual recognition and survival. Malinowski noted that the people who lived on several islands drew closer together as a society because they had established a ring of trust through kula. Everybody within that society formed what they called the kula ring. When a fisherman needed a canoe he could borrow one from somebody within the network. This network assured that he had the means to transport his goods or food to the rest of the island circle. Without the canoe he could not fulfill his obligation to his family or the people. This reciprocal spirit helped to sustain the people of the South Sea Islands, Malinowski noted, a discovery for which he is famous.

There are countless other such accounts of gift giving and gift-giving practices among different peoples. R. Jon McGee and Richard L. Warms (1996) write in their introduction to Marcel Mauss's 1925 study, *The Gift*, that Mauss describes the rules of "generosity on the Andaman Islands and the kula trade in Melanesia, as well as other associated exchange practices." These exchanges, they write, "are the material expressions of Emile Durkheim's social facts. They are used to forge and maintain alliances, and they replicate the divisions between the people involved in them. The interdependence of the exchange network increases social solidarity" (p. 103).

People often depend on such exchanges to remain a people and to keep a strong social bond. The Kiowas had found a way to do that in order to ensure that they knew and remembered who they were, and they still practice it today at powwows and at Carnegie Park every Fourth of July, or anywhere else they gather and can see this outward sign of tribal unity. The practice of kula and other exchanges and gift giving are the means by which cultures bond and continue as social entities (Malinowski 1922; Mauss 1990).

For Kiowas, gift giving or gift exchange occurs in a spirit of goodwill.

My father explained it to me this way: "You give these things because it makes you feel good to do it," he said. "It's not because you want something back. No. Somebody gives you something and you give it away because somebody else is going to feel good that you recognized them. Or else why give them something?"

I thought this over a good many times while doing storytelling fieldwork. I worried that I was somehow supposed to give back to the people I was interviewing and whose stories I recorded, but I didn't know how to proceed. I worried that I needed to reciprocate for these gifts. I worried that I needed to exchange something for their work and participation. One of the ways I learned that I could fulfill my obligation was simply to listen to what they had to say and to let them express themselves and interpret their stories. It wasn't out of the question to allow my consultants to examine the written text and rewrite where necessary. Collaborative ethnography is an excellent recent development in fieldwork, I had read. It allows, among other things, for the ethnographer and consultant to work together throughout the field study (Tedlock 1991, Lawless 1992, Lassiter 2000). After writing and rewriting the text, the ethnographer and consultant or consultants may reassess what has taken place as a kind of follow-up to the complete work. Kiowas often impart information freely, but they expect at least a fair hearing. Listening respectfully and closely is a way of showing that what you are hearing is acceptable and meaningful. It helps to fill the need of ceremony, as Lewis Hyde (1983) has pointed out in his work on gifts and gift giving.

My mother was only reminding me of what was expected of me while I worked with Kiowas, my own people. I came to know immediately what she was talking about each time she told me how Kiowas do things. She was helping me to make sure that I was doing the right Kiowa thing. She was making sure that in fact I was doing a collaborative ethnography. "Do it the Kiowa way," she had declared more than a few times. "That's the right way. That's what counts. That's being Kiowa." When she prepared an elaborate meal for Uncle Oscar and me one day when I first began to interview him and record his stories, that was an exchange gift she made in my behalf. At the time I'd all but forgotten what she was doing and why.

Introduction

It seemed quite unnecessary to go through such elaborate preparation just so I could meet with Uncle Oscar to talk about Kiowa storytelling. At first, I thought there was some other reason she was preparing that big meal. But it was perfectly Kiowa, and I did not for some reason recognize it. Maybe it had been too long since I had experienced this Kiowa way. She didn't explain it to me at the time. Rather, she told me about it later on when we visited. That she had been thinking for a long time about the interview I had planned came up in our talk. Getting wind of it, she had decided to prepare the meal because she recognized how important it was for us and her own tribal self. What she was doing was paying homage to the oldest surviving cousin in her family: Uncle Oscar, her brother in the Kiowa way, was coming to her house. This was a special sign to her. It meant reinforcing family relationships. When she told me it was the Kiowa way of doing things, she was in fact telling me how important it was to reinforce and reaffirm Kiowa-ness, the same sort of spirit I was to experience in storytelling. "You do for your own people because in a way it's expected of you," she said. "Kiowas do it that way. They used to. You don't see that kind of custom anymore. It's just about all gone these days."

She was right, I thought. You didn't see Kiowas treat each other the way they used to when I was a boy. Things were definitely different. My mother did a very ceremonial thing in recognition of this important cultural or tribal event that was about to take place in her home. It was a perfect act, an appropriate time and event in Kiowa life. And it was done well.

Since gift exchange is such an important symbolic act of humans, I believe a little more explanation is needed here. I do not mean to make a symbolic interpretation of Kiowa ritual because that would involve more study and analysis than I can undertake here. What I want to explain is that Kiowas who are told a story recognize the event by an outward sign or some symbolic act of sorts. Victor Turner (1967), for instance, observes that symbols are essential to social processes: "Symbols, as I have said, produce action, and dominant symbols tend to become focuses in interaction. Groups mobilize around them, worship before them, perform other symbolic activities near them, and add other symbolic objects to them, often to make composite shrines" (pp. 93–111). From this standpoint one could argue anthropologically that by gift giving or exchange Kiowas are externalizing some internal social process or interaction. Turner contends that "the symbol becomes associated with human interests, purposes, ends, and means, whether these are explicitly formulated or have to be inferred from the observed behavior. The structure and properties of a symbol become those of a dynamic entity, at least within its appropriate context of action" (pp. 93–111). In other words, Kiowas, through an exchange of a gift, or in my mother's case preparing an elaborate feast, generally show outwardly that some ceremony or ritual is taking place culturally, is approved, and is acceptably Kiowa. Without this outward sign the event being acknowledged would not be recognizably Kiowa.

A social frame or social context surrounds every human performance, as J. Gumperz (1982) has argued. We are told that all humans make these outward acknowledgments. We do so to help each other understand one another. In other words, we humans cannot escape our social context. We are dependent upon our social milieu to come to terms with ourselves, others, and our surroundings (Goffman 1974). Indeed, when we lecture, tell stories, dance, or do just about any social thing, we have to rely on everything around us to impart information about what we are doing and why. Social animals that we are, we have all agreed wittingly or not what social cues or codes are necessary to impart information to one another. We have to rely on this system of social practice in order to make sense of and be understood by the people who share their lives with us in meaningful ways. We may perform the most exacting or ceremonial acts, not even recognizing that they have become so routine that they are as reflexive as breathing air or drinking water (Goffman 1974; Turner 1967). Kiowas, in the exchange of stories, need some outward sign to show that something significant has taken place, that it is no small matter to do these things. These exchanges, in the Durkheimian social sense, are used to forge and maintain alliances, and they reinforce the social bonding between the people involved in them. Without them there is no social entity.

Introduction

The tribe disintegrates into a meaningless heap. As Marcel Mauss (1990) has pointed out:

Material and moral life, as exemplified in gift exchange, function there in a manner at once interesting and obligatory. Furthermore, the obligation is expressed in myth and imagery, symbolically and collectively; it takes the form of interest in the objects exchanged; the objects are never completely separated from the men who exchange them; the communion and alliance they establish are well-nigh indissoluble. The lasting influence of the objects exchanged is a direct expression of the manner in which sub-groups within segmentary societies of an archaic type are constantly embroiled with and feel themselves in debt to each other. (Excerpt, chaps. 2 and 4)

To elaborate more fully is not necessary for our purposes here. I merely want to point out what seems to be going on in gift giving and exchanges so that I can delineate Kiowa storytelling. To be sure, contemporary Kiowa storytelling seems to occur when small, intimate groups of relatives and close friends come together. Many of the stories concern family members, and most tend to be informative and entertaining. Joking and teasing are chief features in Kiowa storytelling. Finally, the contemporary tales in this book are rendered mostly in English, due to the decline in spoken Kiowa.

Although it is not easy to delineate storytelling or categorize Kiowa storytellers, it is even more difficult to explain how storytelling happens. I have already pointed out one way. That is, Kiowas tell stories among people who know each other, because it is easier for a storyteller to talk and to frame a story with people he or she knows. Second, Kiowas reinforce their relationships with other Kiowas when they tell stories. This reinforcement is especially apparent among the small groups of family members and close friends. Some of the narratives become what I call classical oral literature. They become refined in sound, in the repetition of certain key words and phrases, in the way the characters look and talk. There are so many other narrative features found in classical Western literature that also appear in Kiowa stories that I cannot begin to elaborate on them. I have been struck, for example, by similar elements in Homeric verses and Kiowa stories, and in this book I try to bring such discoveries to the attention of those who might be interested. In some not-too-distant future there will be, I am sure, much scholarship conducted on the literary elements in indigenous poetry and storytelling that will corroborate what I can only suggest here.

This book then is more or less a discourse on how Kiowas tell stories. Chapter 1 is an overview of Kiowa oral storytelling. Chapter 2 focuses on the storytelling tradition of Kiowas as it has come down to us. Contemporary oral storytelling constitutes chapter 3, and the remaining chapters consist of story texts and discourses assembled over two and a half years of fieldwork. Finally, readers will find an appendix of narratives rendered in Kiowa. These line-by-line transcriptions match the English translations throughout the book.

Pronunciation Guide for Kiowa

This pronunciation guide will, among other things, give some clue about how Kiowa sounds. It is taken in part from the linguistic work of Laurel Watkins and Parker McKenzie, and I hope it will make the reading of Kiowa easier and enjoyable. Everything I know about Kiowa grammar and Kiowa writing, I learned from Watkins and McKenzie.

Consonants

There are twenty-two consonants in the Kiowa language. Fourteen of these have the same sound as those in English. Eight are distinctive consonantal sounds for which there are no English counterparts. McKenzie lists those sounds as: c, ch, f, j, q, th, x, and v; these include two variants of k/ p/ t, unaspirated and ejective, which he refers to as "soft" and "plosive," and affricatives ejective x and voiceless ch.

The McKenzie Writing System consonants are arranged in the following way:

LANGUAGE GUIDE A

McKenzie Writing System for Consonants

	Labial	Dental	Alveolar	Palatal	Velar	Laryngeal
Stops						
Ejective	v	th			q	
Aspirated	p	t			k	
Unaspirated	f	j			c	
Voiced	b	d			g	
Affricatives						
Ejective			x			
Voiceless			ch			
Fricatives						
Voiceless			s			h
Voiced			z			
Nasal	m	n				
Liquid			l			
Glide				y		w

The McKenzie alphabet features single and two-letter combinations for sounds for which there are no equivalents in English. For example, c, ch, f, j, q, th, v, x represent Kiowa sounds and not those commonly associated in the English alphabet. McKenzie's approach is practical, as he has said, and conveniently utilizes the keys on a typewriter or computer.

p, t, k

The first group of sounds are pronounced exactly as they are in English.

LANGUAGE GUIDE B

	English	Kiowa word	English gloss
p	paint, pinon, poem	pân	sky
		pí	fire
		pói	lice
t	toy, tail, Tony	têm	break
		tén	heart
		tón	tail
k	key, king, klutz	káu:dáu	blanket
		kîn	cough
		kó̠:gí	grandfather

f, j, c

These letters are unaspirated sounds. The corresponding sounds occur in English following S as shown below.

LANGUAGE GUIDE C

	English	Kiowa word	English gloss
f	spike, spit	fâi	sun
		fí̠:gá	food
		fôl	insect
j	stick, stone	jó:dé	shoe
		já̠:	star
		jó̠:	house
c	skate, scarf	Cáuigú	Kiowas
		cí	meat
		cúyàul	coyote

ch

This diphthong has a very special sound in Kiowa. The corresponding English sound usually occurs like the plural S after T, as in cats.

LANGUAGE GUIDE D

English		Kiowa word	English gloss
ch	bats, hits	chę̄	horse
		chát	door
		chói	coffee

---

v, th, q, x

This last group of Kiowa sounds has no equivalent sound in English. They make an explosive sound at the beginning of a word. Linguists refer to these sounds as ejectives.

LANGUAGE GUIDE E

	English	Kiowa word	English gloss
v		váu	creek, moon
		vé	laugh
th		tháp	deer
		thên	hail
		Tháukáui	White person
q		qóp	mountain
		qí	husband
		qáu	knife
x		xól	plume
		xó	stone, rock
		xé	thick
		xân	trick

Pronunciation Guide

The Palatal Glide

In Kiowa, when the consonants /c/, /g/, /k/, or /q/ precede the vowels /a/ or /ai/, there is a *y* sound, so that ca is pronounced *cya*, ga is pronounced *gya*, ka is pronounced *kya*, and qa is pronounced *qya*. Although the McKenzie system does not include the glide marking in the environment where it occurs, it is understood to be there nonetheless. Some Kiowa words where the palatal glide occurs are:

Kiowa word	Pronounced	English
qá̱:hį̱	k'yá̱:hį̱	man
kâi:gùn	kʰyáy:gùn	jump
Câigù	kyâygù	Comanche
cúngà	kúngyà	dance

Vowels

There are ten vowel elements in Kiowa, six vowels and four diphthongs, which may be classified as unnasalized vowels, unnasalized diphthongs, nasalized vowels, and nasalized diphthongs.

The McKenzie Writing System lists them:

Vowel	Pronunciation
i	ee
e	ay
a	ah
o	oh
au	aw
ai	ahy
ui	ooy
oi	owy
aui	awy

Suprasegmentals

All the vowels (v) and diphthongs may be high, low, or high/low, with combinations of length and nasalization, except high/low, which does not need length.

LANGUAGE GUIDE F

1.	Tone		
		high	v́
		low	v̀
		high/low	v̂
2.	Length		v̄, v:
3.	Nasal		<u>v</u>

Pronunciation Guide

The International Phonetic Alphabets (IPA) of Kiowa Phonemes

Below are the IPA corresponding Kiowa phonemes as shown by Watkins.

LANGUAGE GUIDE G

	Labial	Dental	Alveolar	Palatal	Velar	Laryngeal
Stops						
Ejective	p'	t'			k'	
Aspirated	pʰ	tʰ			kʰ	
Unaspirated	p	t			k	(?)
Voiced	b	d			g	
Affricatives						
Ejective			c'			
Voiceless			c			
Fricatives						
Voiceless			s			h
Voiced			z			
Nasal	m	n				
Liquid			l			
Glide				y		w

Telling
Stories
the Kiowa Way

Chapter I
Kiowas and Kiowa Texts

Kiowas are said to have left the Montana high country of the Yellowstone after 1682. James Mooney (1898) places the Kiowas here, as do Elsie Parsons (1929) and William Meadows (1999). By this time they had acquired horses and moved out onto the Great Plains (Mooney 1898, Boyd 1983, Meadows 1999). Most of the literature describes this era as the time of "a dispute over an animal killed on a hunt," when "a portion of the tribe separated and went away to the north never to be heard from again" (Meadows 1999). Tribal legend refers to the incident and breaking up of the tribe as Áu:zài:thàu:hòp (The-Udder-Angry-Ones). According to that legend, the ones who stayed in the north are apparently still there. There have been reports of a strange tribe that speaks a language similar to Kiowa somewhere in Canada, but no one has yet verified the reports. If they had been true, I am sure the Kiowas would have known who the people were and made contact.

According to legend, the Kiowas journeyed eastward into the Black Hills of South Dakota. From here they ventured southward into Wyoming near Devil's Tower. By now they had acquired Táimê, the sun dance medicine, and become a sun dance culture. Benjamin Kracht (1997) describes the sun dance as the "most important Kiowa dance," one that unified the tribe socially and spiritually. By now, they had entered into what is now Kansas and Colorado and, very shortly after, Oklahoma, always on the lookout for the best opportunities, a better place to make camp. Meadows (1999) contends that by the time the Kiowas settled on the southern Plains "they possessed many of the sociocultural forms considered typical of nineteenth-century Plains Indians and were well adapted to a mobile hunting-and-raiding economy which emphasized the horse, tipi, and bison" (p. 34). I should like to add that although the Kiowas are noted for raiding, their real passion was to journey out on the land and take in the full breadth of that magical place. Scott Momaday (1969) describes this period as "a time of great adventure and nobility and fulfillment" (p. 3). "Taime came to the Kiowas in a vision born of suffering and despair," he writes. "Take me with you," T<u>ái</u>mê said, "and I will give you whatever you want" (pp. 3–4).

I like to think of this time as the most adventurous period in Kiowa history. And it was, as Momaday and others have said, a Golden Age of the Kiowa people. The journey they recalled in story continues to be recalled today, and the journey legend is reinforced with every telling. "The journey is an evocation of three things," Momaday writes: "a landscape that is incomparable, a time that is gone forever, and the human spirit, which endures" (p. 4). I like to think about the Kiowas and their place in the world. It is an enduring story, full of meaning and great human value.

The Kiowa Language

Kiowas speak a language similar to those dialects spoken in the Southwest, New Mexico and Arizona. John Harrington, who is credited for detailing much of the structure of the Tanoan languages, noted the similarities between Kiowa and the Pueblo languages as early as 1923. In *The Pueblo Indian World* (Hewett and Dutton 1945), he notes that a "considerable study of the various Pueblo Indian languages of the Southwest and of the Kiowa language of the Great Plains area, amounting to a very detailed study of some of these, reveals that all of these languages without exception are closely genetically related one to another and to the Aztec, also called Nahuatl, of central Mexico" (p. 157). By the time of this writing, other linguists have tried to categorize Indian languages everywhere. Although some have categorized Kiowa as Caddoan or Algonkian, others cannot place it in any language family and have simply relegated it to the category of "isolate."

Because Harrington decided to eliminate what he terms the "niceties of Indian pronunciation," he provides "an approximation" of the vowel and consonant sounds of the Pueblo and Kiowa languages as a kind of announcement of what he has discovered in the Southwest. He seems reluctant to call attention to this matter, for it had always been a source of much argument among linguists of his day. Unfortunately, his announcement went almost unnoticed until he brought out a more inclusive Kiowa study a few years later, assisted by the late Parker McKenzie.[1] Of that publication McKenzie writes that "as an honor gesture, [Harrington] included me as co-author, although I took no part in its preparation. He never learned I was much disappointed my Kiowa writing system was not used in it, but I recognized he intended the monograph for linguists and therefore had to use a writing system they would understand" (McKenzie Notes and Correspondences, n.d., n. pag.).

I knew personally of his disappointment and wish Harrington had included McKenzie's writing system. I became aware of the system around 1980 when I worked at the Kiowa tribal compound in Carnegie. By then, others had also taken notice of the system and were commenting on its uniqueness and practicality. Because there were still many questions about Kiowa grammar at the time, McKenzie's invention did not receive the attention it deserved until 1998, when the tribe itself initiated the Kiowa Language Preservation Program and officially adopted the system in its teaching component.

With the publication of Laurel Watkins's *Grammar of Kiowa* (1984), many of the major problems of Kiowa grammar were settled. That work was also achieved with the assistance of Parker McKenzie and is perhaps the most influential one on Kiowa to date. Beginning with a fine introduction, it outlines Kiowa phonology, morphology, and syntax. This work, like Harrington's, stands as a testimony to the importance of the attempts to understand an American Indian language. The struggle to keep native languages alive is a major concern not only for scholars but for tribes themselves. It is the combined efforts of both scholars and tribe members—especially storytellers—that will ensure the survival of indigenous languages and make them a living part of Indian communities across the country in the years to come.

A Storytelling Ethnography

In my storytelling fieldwork, I learned or relearned how Kiowas tend to respond to questions. Once I asked John Tofpi, my major storytelling consultant, why Kiowa stories sounded better at night. He smiled and nodded his head, as he is prone to do at times, but he said nothing. I sensed that this was his way of showing that I was probably right. He often responded to my questions with silence during our work together. I don't think he did this because he didn't know how to answer. Indeed, his silence was an apt answer to such questions. Not answering directly often meant that he needed time to muse. He wasn't about to answer without giving my question a good going-over. Cornelius Spottedhorse reacted the same way, as did Dorothy Kodaseet, my two other consultants. Dorothy was especially shy about answering questions. Sometimes she would simply say she didn't know. Or would keep silent. She must have thought it strange of me to ask about how Kiowas told stories. It must have been unsettling for her, and I'm not so sure she didn't think me a rather odd fellow sometimes. I would have to go back later and pose the same question or rephrase it, but each time I did I was rewarded, sometimes with more than I had dreamed, for she might expand her answer.

"Dorothy, are Kiowas prone to tell stories to their own grandchildren?"

Put another way: "Dorothy, how often did your grandfather tell you stories when you were a little girl?" Or: "Dorothy, who told you stories? Your parents or grandparents?"

I remember quite a few times a smile would light up her face as if she'd suddenly recalled a special moment a long time ago when things were easier and there was so much to live for. "He told me stories. Yes, he used to go to the store and buy *ésán* [sweet food stuff]. Grandpa."

"He did?"

"My aunt was jealous too. She used to watch everything we did together."

"Why?"

"She thought we were getting too much attention. I don't know. I loved my grandpa."

Dorothy was very fond of her grandparents, especially her grandfather, I-See-O. I-See-O was one of the famous Kiowa Indian scouts attached to the 7th Cavalry under Hugh L. Scott. Scott befriended I-See-O. They were very close, I am told. One time, during the Spanish American War, Scott asked his old friend to prepare a special prayer for his safe return from that war. He had been assigned overseas. I-See-O took the general into a sweat lodge he had built himself and prayed for him before the Tàlídàui, sacred medicine bundle, which he kept.[2] Scott returned safely, wounded only in the hand. Later on, he became chief of staff in Washington, D.C. He never forgot I-See-O or the special prayer for his safe return.

On a return visit to the Kiowa Elders Center I would sometimes find Dorothy ready to answer a question I had posed earlier. I'd find her busy working at the reception desk or in the dining room. Painfully shy, she would hardly look up at me when approached.

When she finally finished whatever she was doing, however, she would sit down quietly, fold her hands together, and answer my questions as best she could. Sometimes, she'd tell me another story about I-See-O. She once told me about the time her own father had to carry the Tàlídàui medicine bundle on horseback from Fort Sill to his home west of Carnegie, about a forty-mile ride. The horse died before they reached home, she said.

"My father had to carry that medicine strapped to his back," she said. "It was heavy but he brought it home."

"Did he ever explain to you why the horse died?" I asked.

"No."

"How did it die?"

She paused for a long time. In typical Kiowa fashion she seemed to search the depths of her consciousness for the right answer. "I don't know. It just died. It was hot that day."

I didn't ask her any more questions. She seemed to be satisfied with the amount of information she had given. When I asked her later on about that incident, she offered another detail. This time she told me exactly where the incident occurred.

"It was up near Fred Botone's. Do you know where that old house is?"

"Yes," I answered. "I do."

"It was there. That horse just dropped dead right there. For no reason. I don't know why it died like that. You know, they used to carry the medicine on the back of a horse then. Horses never died like that."

"How did the medicine come to be in your father's possession?"

"My grandpa I-See-O died at Fort Sill. Them soldiers built him a house there. He was my father's father-in-law. My father had to take care of the medicine."

I knew what she was talking about. If your parent is a keeper and dies and you are the oldest son, it is generally left up to you to take over as keeper. When my grandfather died, because he had no son, my mother had to assume the responsibilities of keeper of the Tàlídàui. She looked to me for help whenever she needed it because I was the oldest grandson. I knew how to smoke the pipe and transport the medicine when it was required.

It was difficult, as I say, but I persisted asking questions about Kiowa storytelling, and all of my consultants tried to provide me answers. In time, I thought I was getting better at asking questions. Sometimes I would drive home and be thinking about what I would ask next. Sometimes at home a good question would come up in my mind, and I would have to stop whatever I was doing and sit down and write it out. I wanted to know everything I could about Kiowa storytelling. Like Keith Basso (1990), I wanted to focus "on a small set of spoken texts in which members of a contemporary American Indian society express claims about themselves, their language, and the lands on which they live" (p. 100). I didn't know there were going to be surprises in store for me. In the course of my study, I also found out a lot about myself, not because I was a student in the field of ethnography and native languages but because I was another person trying to make sense out of the conditions people are born into and live all of their lives in and trying to explain why things happen as they do, things like growing old, becoming infirm or ill, and dying. I, too, was a part of this human drama, I realized, whether I liked it or not. In short, the many conversations I had and recordings I made in the time I spent in the field revealed more about the Kiowa people than I had ever expected. But the experience also allowed me to peer into a place within myself where my own tribal sense of well-being and wholeness resided. And almost as if by accident, I began to think about being Kiowa and what it meant to me in relation to the world around me. Somehow, like a storyteller, I was providing a frame around my own existence, my own life.

Something else: Having grown up Kiowa and played an active role in Kiowa life as a boy, I had taken my Kiowa heritage for granted, as I know many Kiowas still do. I had assumed I knew all there was to know about life and living it. I had not intended to make much of the fact that I was Kiowa. Indeed, I think I actively tried to extricate myself from my Kiowa identity a few times. I had lived in that culture and spoken the Kiowa language, although not fluently from early childhood. After I grew older and left home, I had all but forgotten the world of the Kiowas. Every now and then the memory of the pleasant sound of Kiowa words or the recollection of a story came to me, and I became either sad or happy. Other times a familiar image from childhood would crop up in my mind as I was writing or speaking or dreaming and send me on another journey of remembrance and longing. And still other times I would be caught off guard and utter a Kiowa word or phrase to an old acquaintance I happened to meet on the street or in some odd place like a movie house or grocery store.

I believe I have heard some of the best old Kiowa stories over the years. And I further believe that I wouldn't know as much as I do about the Kiowa language and oral tradition if it weren't for all the raconteurs, mythmakers, poets, madmen, and saints who surrounded my life at one time or another as I was growing up. I am grateful to them, but I am especially indebted to my grandfather and Kiowa relatives who took the time to tell me what it was or what it took to be a Kiowa person. They weren't telling me how to behave or to do this or do that. Far from it. They just wanted me to stay true to my own heart and try to stay on the straight road. That was it.

The old stories, my Kiowa relatives, and all the things that had made so much sense to me and which I embraced a long time ago suddenly became part of my life again. The realization, or how it came home to me, was both surprising and dramatic. I stayed in Kiowa country for about six years and left. Ten years later I returned again to do the fieldwork that produced this book. The lapse of time between when I first moved back home, left, and returned again had caused me to reassess what Kiowa traditions and customs were. I cannot say I know or understand all there is to know about Kiowas or what makes Kiowas who they are. I can say only that much of what Kiowas care about can be found in their closeness as families and relatives, their songs, dances, rituals, and stories. When I began to interview and record the stories that became a part of this book years later, I had a chance to think more about what it was to be a Kiowa and what being Kiowa meant to me. I thought how the values I learned and grew up with had affected me, how they informed the narratives I was collecting and trying to analyze.

To do the fieldwork I needed to record a choice of narratives that I thought best exemplified Kiowa storytelling in modern times. I tried as earnestly as I could to select consultants who not only spoke Kiowa but were also knowledgeable about the culture and traditions of the tribe. Because I wanted to do as collaborative an ethnography as possible, I chose consultants who were not afraid to talk or ask questions. One of these was Oscar Tsoodle, a close relative of mine.

When I began looking around for people to help me figure out what was going on when Kiowas told stories, I had a lot of these things on my mind. The sense of Kiowa tribal unity was falling apart, our spoken language was in rapid decline, but I was determined to work as hard as I could to bring together something that gave us some clue about oral narratives, and that's when I put even greater effort into locating Kiowas whom I thought were still master speakers in the old way.

Working in Close with People

Who were the Kiowa master speakers in the late twentieth century? The late Oscar Tsoodle was one, and perhaps even the last traditional Kiowa peyote practitioner.[3] The other, Parker McKenzie, was a Kiowa linguist in every sense of the word because he was self-taught. Truly one of a kind. In my opinion, McKenzie's work in Kiowa is incomparable and always will be. No Kiowa I know has ever achieved his understanding of or his ability to explain the most minute parts of Kiowa. He did everything he could to teach me how the language worked and even recorded several stories for me the summer before he died. He knew as well as any Kiowa elder that the language was in decline. He, more than any Kiowa, could speak the truth about its possible death. And he tried very hard to show every living Kiowa that if each individual took a real interest in the language it had a chance of surviving a little longer in this world. In addition to the help of Uncle Oscar and Parker, I had the assistance of my storytelling consultants and others in the discipline. Thanks to them I believe I am learning how to do better fieldwork and how to assemble an ethnographic study of oral storytelling. Furthermore, I have learned that, although many of the old stories are being lost, new ones—in fact, great contemporary narratives—turn up in Kiowa country all the time.

Another thought I need to add here: I am in awe of the ability of humans to create and re-create stories and tell them the same way they did centuries ago. In order to see how this was done I had to record and interview as many of the living storytellers as I could in Kiowa country. I had worked with the Kiowa tribe in the early nineties. I learned as much Kiowa in that span as perhaps I had hearing it and speaking it in a Kiowa home long ago. I say again that I am grateful to grandparents who spoke only Kiowa around the house and insisted that I understand and respond as much as I could in the same language, even though we were also an English-speaking bunch and could converse as well as anyone outside. You could say "bring the water," "sit down," "go outside," "how are you feeling," in Kiowa. Spoken Kiowa was as natural a part of our lives as breathing air.

Asking the Right Questions

I asked myself not a few times out in the field whether the questions I was putting to my storytelling consultants were relevant or made any kind of sense. Were they the proper questions one asked Kiowas? Was there such a thing as a Kiowa storyteller? If so, how was it determined? What about the tradition of storytelling? Was there one? How old was it? Did it just consist of stories heard in Kiowa and then told to the next generation for posterity? Were contemporary Kiowas telling stories the same way their forbears had a century back? What system was there for telling stories? How much did it draw on tribal customs and values?

My consultants had never before been asked such questions. They must have thought I was acting "too much like a white man," their usual assessment of someone who asks questions that aren't commonly asked. They must have considered me foolish for behaving out of the ordinary Kiowa order of things. As far as they were concerned, one consultant told me, "We simply tell stories and that is it. We don't memorize them. We don't try to make them fancy like white people do. Who cares?" Yes, I thought. Who cares how they, contemporary Kiowas, tell stories anyway? Who needs to know? Kiowa storytelling seems pretty obvious if you just sit down and listen. It helps to be Kiowa and to know a little Kiowa. You tell stories because they keep you alive. Stories keep alive the hopes, aspirations, and dreams of the tribe, just as they did in the old days. What is so unusual about that?

Yes, sometimes I felt pretty foolish. Not because of all of the questions I asked but because I was a Kiowa too; and what business did I have of asking my own people these things? Let the white man do that. He is expected to do such things. Not a fellow Kiowa.

But still, in the end, the fieldwork was rewarding. I learned a great deal about Kiowa storytelling, and am still learning. I also learned how to think carefully about questions that were asked of me before I answered them, the correct Kiowa way. Kiowas communicated not only during ordinary conversation but during rounds of storytelling. There was always time to think and reflect, comment and interpret while telling or listening to stories. Every time I sat down and recorded and interviewed consultants, I expected to spend most of an afternoon doing it. I knew there would be an almost equal time of pausing, thinking, and reflection. Many non-Indians I believe would find this exasperating. I can now see why someone like Elsie Clews Parsons (1929) could get so upset doing fieldwork with Kiowas.[4] Like the traditional storytellers of old, contemporary Kiowa storytellers tell fantastic tales that could be true or untrue. Dennis Tedlock (1983) observes that when the Zunis tell fictional stories "they do recognize certain kinds of truth in them" (p. 164), and they often make "etiological claims" in the closings.

The sun sometimes has a halo now, and deer are now capable of witchcraft and must therefore be hunted with special precautions. Asked whether this tale were true, Andrew Peynetsa said, "Almost. That's why the sun is that way;" asked on another occasion whether this narrative was a *telapnanne* [tale, italics mine], he said, "Yes, it's a telapnanne, and after the telapnanne was acted the deer became all wicked." Joseph Peynetsa, asked whether this tale really happened, said, "No. I say no, but I don't know why the hunters do this. Somewhere, somebody must have found out. Somehow, maybe an accident. Maybe it wasn't like this, but later something must have happened to make people think the deer were witches. Anyway, all the hunters know this." (pp. 164–65)[5]

Stories That Could Be True

It is often hard to tell the difference between fiction and nonfiction in old and contemporary Kiowa stories. According to the dictionary, something is verisimilar when it has the appearance of truth or reality. Dennis Tedlock, who has worked with Zuni storytellers for many years, had constantly to ask whether this or that tale really happened because the storytellers employed verisimilitude as a narrative device. "Though it is true that Zunis generally regard their telapnaawe (tales told only at night and during winter)," he writes, "they do recognize certain kinds of 'truth' in them, often citing etiological claims in the closings" (p. 164). He goes on to observe that "explanatory elements, then, since they refer to real conditions, lend an air of reality to the stories that lead to them. This is para-logism," he writes, "a literary device described by Aristotle: 'Whenever, if A is or happens, a consequent, B, is or happens, men's notion is that, if the B is, the A also is. . . . Just because we know the truth of the consequent, we are in our own minds led on to the erroneous inference of the truth of the antecedent.'[6] Faulty logic it may be, but Aristotle approved of it as a verisimilitudinal device" (p. 164). Tedlock mentions that one of the highest compliments paid a Zuni storyteller is that he tells a story "as if he were actually there."[7]

In my own work with contemporary Kiowa storytellers, I was told on several occasions that so-and-so can tell a story "like it's real." The account of how T<u>á</u>imê came to the Kiowas, as told by my grandfather (chapter 3), is a good example. I use the terms verisimilitude, magic realism, and fantastic fairly interchangeably when I describe how Kiowas tell stories because there is a mixture of these devices in many of the narratives and we as yet do not know how exactly to distinguish one from the other. Let me just say that any time these terms come up there is a possibility that one or several of these devices are being employed by the narrator. One day John Tofpi told me a story that could have been a dream or a real incident.

"It was a hand," he said. "I saw a hand and I heard a voice speaking." He said the voice told him things about his life and things about the living world. "It was giving me something," he continued.

I didn't know what to make of the story and didn't know the proper way to ask him how to explain it. It would have been rude if I had. It would have been an insult to ask him if it was a dream or something real, so I didn't say anything.

"It held out its hand and I reached like this for it. It was in the shape of a tree, just like that one down by that bridge. I went down there and I looked around for it and I found it. That tree. It was in the shape of a hand."

I listened to his story with real interest, because I thought I recognized so many familiar things in it. It seemed clear to me that he was recounting a real event. Something had come to help him live a better life. After all, didn't everything change for the better after the dream?

I had to agree that he must have had a true revelation. Kiowas present stories that, like good fiction, have aspects of the real and the unreal. There is little separation between what happened and what might have happened, and the storyteller does not reveal such distinctions. This kind of storytelling frame keeps the listener involved intimately in the tale, under the storyteller's spell, so to speak. My grandfather told what most non-Indians would term fantastic tales because the content was so unbelievable. He had somehow learned the art or aesthetics of telling a story this way to intensify the dramatic effects. Like any good Kiowa storyteller, he had learned that you could build up a powerful plot and action by making the listener believe things that were otherwise unbelievable. He had cultivated the skill common to all good storytellers, the skill of keeping listeners engaged.

Special storytelling devices and the heavy use of supernatural occurrences are what initially drew my attention to the early Greek myths. At the time I wondered if Homer wasn't himself a Kiowa, because, like the Kiowas, he heard voices and talked to inanimate things like rocks, trees, and ocean waves. Julian Jaynes (1976) writes about the primitive stage of human consciousness when the brain was "bicameral" and producing uncontrollable "voices" attributed to the gods. Could there have been such a time when Kiowas were hearing the same voices? And do these voices show up in Kiowa oral narratives as they supposedly do in many of the ancient Greek texts and the Bible?

In one aspect, oral storytelling is itself poetry, or at least a kind of poetry. There are certain features in poetry that suggest orality and storytelling. For one, poetry has as its source the spoken word. Poetry from its inception was an oral undertaking and so has always been connected with the word uttered. Most poets would in fact rather have their poems heard than read in print. The very early association of poetry and spoken words roots poetry in the kind of orality of which Jaynes speaks.

Let me go a little farther to explain. To a poet, there is a certain attraction and fascination for language and words. Many poets have attributed their ability to make poems to some realm of the mind or imagination they describe as "primeval," "wild," "passionate" or some state of being I have heard described as "early human consciousness" and a vital creative link without which a poet could not produce a good poem. It is often difficult, if not frustrating, for the hard-core academic mind to relate to this area of creativity. The ability to write a poem is metaphysical and cannot in most cases be challenged successfully in an academic way and therefore has always been a source of much misunderstanding between the arts and academia. Somehow or another, poets and people attracted to the spoken word and the magic therein seem to be in touch with something otherworldly that the rest of humanity is not. Consider what the poets Kim Addonizio and Dorriane Laux (1997) say about how poems seemingly "come to us as gifts."

[Carolyn] Kizer was working on a long poem for weeks, unable to make much headway, feeling frustrated and blocked. She kept at it long after she felt she should give up. One morning she sat down at her desk with the poem in front of her, ragged and misshapen as ever, and she was *suddenly struck by inspiration* [italics mine] and wrote a new poem which came quickly and fully. The way she explained it, the muse saw her struggling, determined and committed for days on end and then decided, out of the goodness of her heart, to give her a poem, *gratis*. And of course the poem wasn't really free; Kizer had worked hard for it and was entitled to the fruits of her labor. The poem only felt free, but what a feeling. (p. 203)

Compare Jaynes (1976), who asks in the chapter titled "Of Poetry and Music," "What unseen light leads us to such dark practice? And why does poetry flash with recognitions of thoughts we did not know we had, finding its unsure way to something in us that knows and has known all the time, something, I think, older than the present organization of our nature?" (p. 361).

That poems seemingly come "quickly and fully" to poets is fairly well known, and yet nobody seems to be able to explain how this happens. If we are going to understand Kiowa storytelling, or any non-Western literatures, for that matter, we need to take a very close look at some of the research on orality and literacy, because both have a huge bearing on how we should approach a culture that relies heavily on an oral tradition. One of the biggest problems in scholarship is how we look at something new and different. This is where much of the misunderstanding is, as I see it. I was attracted to Greek literature, and in that attraction I saw that there was a tradition of literature that was produced much as it was among Kiowas. There were many books written on the subject of Greek literature and culture. People had spent countless years studying the Greek myths and writing many volumes on the subject.[8] Everything I learned at one time or another seemed to be based upon the Greek culture model. The very alphabet we had all learned to use was largely a product of the Greeks. At some point I began to wonder, if we could understand and use what the Greeks had produced, why couldn't we do the same thing for Kiowa literature? If we could take Homer's texts and develop them into a Western thought and literature, we could also develop a non-Western literature.

One day John Tofpi and I went out to the Slick Hills for Indian perfume. *Àu:hį:.* Àu:hį: is native juniper. The kind Kiowas like is a special kind of cedar and you don't find it just anywhere. It grows in the rocky hills south of Carnegie. He told me about the three different places to get it. John T. is in my estimation the àu:hį: maven. The two most important clay paints Kiowas use to paint themselves are *gúl:áum:gá* (red paint) and *gùtqógùl:àum:gà* (yellow paint). They are holy paints. Sacred. Many of his stories deal with these subjects. He even conducts tours out to the places where he collects cedar and Indian paints. He must know every location in the area and talks a lot about the different kinds of cedars and paints and where one can find the best. It seems that a great amount of his free time is spent drying and preparing àu:hį:.

That April day John and I went to the Slick Hills was cold, windy. Almost gale-force wind. We drove southward from Carnegie. All along the way he told me stories about cedar and how it is used by Kiowas. He said he thought modern Kiowas had no use for these sacred things and that he thought he should tell them about it whenever he could. He liked to tell people, he said. He even took them to see where the stuff grew and showed them how they had to cut it. It was all pretty ceremonial.

"You have to do these things right," he said.

We parked along the highway. He pointed up the rocky hills. I thought we'd never reach the summit.

"There," he laughed. "Hàu. It's thick up there."

Yes, I nodded my head, regretting I had come out here in this awful cold, not to mention that rocky climb I would soon have to make. If there is a stiff price for everything that is worthwhile and good, this was judgment time, I thought.

We climbed out of the car, while trucks barreled by almost shaking us out of our clothes. We braved the steep granite escarpment and arrived at the summit. The wind was so sharp you could feel it through your clothes and into your bones. I almost turned around and walked back down to the car to wait, but John T.'s time was too important. Besides, he might tell a story and I would miss out on it.

We found small junipers. A stand of them, green and swaying in the wind like long layers of green skirts. They were knotted together on a precipice. It was about a hundred-foot drop from there to flat ground below. As I looked over the edge, I had visions of me plunging headlong down to the ground. I wondered why I had come out here anyway.

"This is it," John announced as soon as we arrived. He took off his cap and prayed quietly. I felt guilty and ashamed for not having more faith in this little field trip that turned out to be one of the most significant moments in my work with him.

I peered out over the granite outcropping. "That's a long ways down."

We cut off branches. Sure enough, when I pinched off a sample of the needles and brought my fingers to my nose the scent was remarkable, unmistakable. It was the right kind of fragrance. It was a prayer fragrance, the kind Kiowas smoked the house with after a death in the family or sprinkled over the open fire in the peyote tipi.

We filled our two grocery bags full and drove home quietly. On the way he told me all about àu:hį́: and *séó:gá*, sweet sage perfume, another special fragrance favored and used ceremonially by Kiowa men. I thought about Indian fragrances for women and could come up with not one. I wondered if women used any kind of special scents at all. I remember making a mental note to ask John later but forgot all about it.

"It's a medicine. It's a prayer, guy. You have to make a prayer before you cut it. When you get home, use it. Don't just let it sit somewhere. If you don't use it right away, give it away to other people or put it in a small sack and spread it around the house so the house smells good. It's a good medicine for these things."

I brought my portion home. I hope to use some of it as he prescribed or give it away as he told me that I should. The point I want to make here is there was a small story about fragrance cedar, but we had to go out and find it first. We had to struggle up the granite slope in the cold wind. We had to make a prayer and then cut the branches and put it in sacks. All this took time. A whole afternoon after lunch. We drove about twelve miles to locate it. On the way home he told me the story of àu:hí:, that it was a prayer, a ceremony. It had all the aspects of a ceremony. The same amount of intensity but in a smaller portion.

Chapter II

Conversations with John Tofpi

I knew where to sit down and pray
because it came to me in that dream.

The Dream Story

Tribal traditions, like the Kiowa language, have been passed down to John Tofpi by his family and the Kiowa tribe. These traditions include praying every day the old Kiowa way, treating one's relatives with care and honor, singing the old songs, and telling stories. If you sit down with John Tofpi, he will invariably talk about the good old days. He will tell you all about his family and other families in the tribe. He will tell about the events he considers important when he was a young Kiowa man growing up, and he will not fail to mention people who were informative and influential to him in life, "who told me how things were." He likes to reminisce and joke about his friends and relatives. Sometimes he is serious; other times he is laughing; he seems always to be having a good time. But most important of all, he is sure that without all of his close relatives he would not have turned out to be the man he is today. He thinks that everything that ever happened to him was meant to be. Things don't just happen, he often tells me.

Chapter II ◎ Conversations with John Tofpi

"You know, things have a meaning," he will say. "There is a reason for everything. You know that?" One day he said:

I was sitting down by that old tree near the bridge where you all live and I saw you and your little boy coming down the road. I was sitting under that tree. I went down there to sit and pray. You know that big tree is shaped funny. [He gestures with his hand, extending it out as if to grasp some object someone is handing him]. I go down there to pray sometimes. That's why I was there that time. Hàu. You and your boy were coming down there. I saw you all. I was just sitting there. I saw that tree. It was kind of big. By the creek there. It's there. You can see it.

He didn't even finish telling me why he was there at that particular location praying until a few weeks later, when I went back to Carnegie and asked him about it again. At the time I didn't know if it was a dream he was relating or a real event. He told about praying under the tree without any explanation or anything, so casually, and the next thing I knew he was finished. He opened the story and stopped, as many Kiowas do when telling stories. We were sitting on the southeast corner of the front lobby at the Kiowa Elders Center where we had been meeting over the course of months since I started interviewing individuals and recording storytelling and stories. It was a windy, cold day outside. Sam Ako, a relative of his, was sitting across from us. Sam, who has had cerebral palsy from birth, has some difficulty getting around normally. His speech isn't very clear, and if you're not used to it you have trouble understanding him. I hadn't known Sam Ako very well when I worked at the Center some years back, but this time we sat down together and talked quite a bit, and I was enjoying our newly established acquaintanceship. At this hour of day there is generally an absence of people. They would be arriving very shortly, I thought, and if I wanted to hear anything important, now was the time. John Tofpi was on a roll. You can hardly keep him from talking when he is in the mood, but he can get a little tongue-tied if you ask him too many intimate questions in front of other people.

"Hàu," he said in a serious tone of voice, after I had asked him several times about the tree and creek incident. "I saw that hand in my dream. It was just like this." He held his hand aloft and spread his fingers in the manner of tree branches. "It came just like this in that dream and said, 'Open your hand. I want to give you something.' Just like that."

He opened his eyes as wide as double barn doors, as he does when he's telling something he considers extraordinary. Kiowas like to hear their listeners make a response, and every so often I had to answer hàu.

"You know that?" He blinked his eyes several times and asked me again. "You know that, guy?"

Hàu. I knew. "Yes, I know it," I repeated.

"I raised up my hand just like this. No, I opened it like this and something fell into it and I shut it. I didn't look at it. But I could feel it in my hand. Just like this."

To illustrate how, he held his clasped hand way up high to show Sam and me how. Sam laughed and looked the other way. He said something in Kiowa.

John T. glanced around at him. "See there?" he said, "That's something, ain't it?"

I looked at Sam. About seventy years old, he sat across from us in one of those overstuffed chairs that were all around in that drafty large front room. He had his legs crossed in front of him. He grinned wide. Toothless. His strong chin, anvil-shaped, stuck out a little from the rest of his face. It was speckled with coarse black and silver whiskers.

"It sure is, ain't it?" I said, to let him know it was all right for him to jump in anytime he wanted to talk.

Sam cackled. He nodded his head in agreement.

"That Sáuibé, he sure has a good story, ain't it?" Sam said in Kiowa to me in a lowered voice, as if he wanted to share something very special with me. I liked the way he did it. I was proud because he was prone not to talk too much to just anybody. I also liked the sound of the Kiowa words Sam spoke. They seemed to open up a new vista to me. I wanted to hear every syllable, every word he uttered once more. I wanted to take it all in right there.

"I don't know what it was," John continued, still speaking in English.

"But when I opened my hand to look at it there was nothing. I looked in my hand and there was nothing there. But I had this image in my mind. I could see it just like that."

"How was it shaped?" I asked him to hear him again. I was dying to ask him if it was a dream or a real event.

"Like that," went John. He held his hand up in the air and spread his fingers. "I saw this image and I knew where it was and because I walked over there by that bridge below your house. You know the one I'm talking about."

"Yes, I know," I said. In order to keep his story going I had to constantly respond that I knew what he was talking about. It's the Kiowa way of following somebody's story, and I knew my response was expected or he might stop right there. You say hàu, yes, to keep the story going. I don't know what would happen if I didn't.

"I sat down right under that tree. I looked around at those other trees but they weren't shaped right. When I saw this one tree I knew that was the one."

"Is that why you sat down under it?"

I was wondering again if I shouldn't ask him if this was all a dream. Not yet, I thought. I wanted him to let me know somehow or another. I was accustomed somewhat to listening to Kiowa stories. I knew how Kiowas told stories, but this time, because I was doing fieldwork on storytelling, I wanted to be absolutely sure that everything that was going on right there was the real thing. But when it came time to jump into the question I needed to ask, I was stumped. I decided to ride it out. The answer to my question, I decided, would have to come when he was ready to let me know. Kiowas by and large like to take their time. They don't like to rush about, talking, thinking, or at least it appears that they don't. Many times while doing fieldwork in Kiowa country I found myself rushing about, going in and out, driving downtown for supplies or food and so forth. Sometimes I would sit down and talk to some Kiowa elder and in the next moment I'd jump up and go and talk with somebody else, and I know I must have driven some of those poor elders crazy. Part of my own frenzy I know is just my own nervous energy. When I compare myself with other

Kiowas, it is as if I am some kind of alien in their midst, and so I find that I have to slow down and try to relax a lot more than I usually do.

"I did," John said. "I knew where I had to sit down and pray because it came to me in that dream."

Aha, I thought. Now I know it was a dream. Let's see what he has to say about that now.

"But what did it mean?" I asked. "That tree in there and all?" I was trying to keep the narrative going as best I could. I sensed that the story was still wide open. At this stage of narration, I'd begun to learn, any participation by a listener is possible and even expected. He was now looking right at me. I didn't know what to expect. I imagine he must have thought it incredible that I could ask such a stupid question. And I felt astonishingly foolish asking it, so I put it another way.

"I mean, Sáuibé, how did it make you feel? What you experienced I mean."

"Who me?" He kind of chuckled. "I guess it meant things were going to be okay. That *He* was going to be with me. You know I was drinking a lot. Too much, boy. I lost my wife and for several years I was lost. I didn't know what to do. I went around aimless all the time."

I wanted to tell him I was sorry, but I knew he wouldn't know how to respond to such a statement. Kiowas, of course, understand English remarks like "thank you," "I'm sorry," "you're welcome," and so on. However, such remarks, in the Kiowa mind anyway, are almost always unnecessary. For Kiowas, they seem empty of any real value or meaning. I have often tried to find some Kiowa equivalent of such things but failed. I had to check myself a good many times out in the field. Even when you're speaking in English to Kiowas you have to maintain a Kiowa sensibility always. I found myself sitting through many sessions with John and others and saying nothing when, on the other hand, I would have been considered insensitive or unsympathetic if I had been sitting with a white person in similar circumstances.

"When did she die?"

"Who? My wife?" He thought about it a minute. "In 1971. January 14."

"That wasn't too long ago."

Chapter II ◎ Conversations with John Tofpi

It grew quiet for a long time. I waited, a bit anxious. Maybe I'd said something wrong, I thought. I should have been more careful. I didn't know what to do but wait. I was about to say something, when all of a sudden, he spoke up again.

"No. It was bad. Gyah." He fixed his glassy eyes on me as if he wanted me to say something. When I didn't, he spoke up himself.

"I stayed away from the drum for five years," he lamented. "I never went near the sound of the drum. A cousin of mine told me not to stay away from this. You might get sick, he told me. Bad, ain't it?"

I thought about how bad it must have been for him. How alone he must have felt living up there in that small house of his at the edge of town. Even now, every time I drove past his house I would glance over at it sitting there in the middle of the lot. It looked the same way it always had when I was a boy. It seemed fastened there permanently to the earth so it wouldn't take to the air mysteriously. I always wondered how it looked inside. Did it have lots of furniture? Or just a table with one chair? Perhaps he owned a bed. A sofa. I was curious. I had visited lots of Indian homes out there, including Parker McKenzie's tiny house out at Mountain View. They're really lonely places.[1] Usually furnished with old furniture. Indians didn't lack in things, I used to think. They just like living the way they do. I think living in simple conditions made them feel more at home, as if life was the way it used to be long ago. You go inside a house sometimes and all the old ghosts rush at you. It's like entering a strange forest, but one that is not scary. It's just different. The forest trees are the same as the ones you know. You look at them and touch them to see why you are so taken by them but still are not sure. I sometimes wonder if I have lived another life and if I am experiencing something from that time and place. Who knows. But as I was saying, when I go by John's house I think about the old times and wonder how he must live alone, and I sometimes ask myself, Does he cook for himself? I wonder how a Kiowa man such as John Tofpi takes care of a house and does all the housework most Kiowa women do. These days most Kiowa women think husband and wife should handle housework pretty much on an equal basis if both work every day, as they generally do. He must have had to eat

25

pretty simply, because I can't picture him frying an egg or boiling coffee. He's probably consumed lots of Campbell's soups.

"So you drank," I said after a few minutes had passed. "I mean I didn't know that you did that."

He stared at me a moment and then looked out the huge front window where some old people were shuffling in the double doors now. It was brighter outside now than earlier, but still chilly. Sunshine streamed in the windows that reached from the floor to ceiling, but there was a brisk north wind blowing. It had rained the day before, and there was a pool or two of clear water standing in the street in front of the large stone building. Every time the doors opened a cold gust of wind blew into the big room, making us sort of hunker down in our chairs as if to hold on and keep from floating into the air. I hoped the wind would let up before I drove home later that day.

"Yeah," John exhaled suddenly to my relief. It was as if he had been holding his breath for a long time. "I was lost, boy. Real lost. You don't know how it is when you lose your mate, guy."

"And so what did that dream mean to you?" I had to be sure it was a dream. I had to be especially certain where the dream left off and reality started. Did he dream the tree and then go looking for it? Or was the tree just one of the manifestations of the dream, like everything that had happened in it, like Jeff, my son, and me walking down the road below our house. Things just were not clear to me yet.

"You mean me?" He gave me the most serious look he'd given me all morning. "It was there to show me. It was there to help me make a prayer so I could go straight maybe. I don't know. But I went down there to pray and sure enough I began to get better. I quit drinking and started to sing, you know."

I couldn't picture him drinking. Didn't want to or couldn't. More than ten years ago when I was working at the Center, I never once saw him appear to have been drinking. Not John Tofpi. That was unimaginable. And now here he was telling me he drank. Back then. I was not so much shocked as I was curious. If you drank around there, everybody knew about it. It was public record, like getting married or divorced or thrown into jail. I had close relatives who were alcoholics, and I'm sure every person in town knew that they were, because people around Carnegie make it their business to know everybody else's. Typical small town. After my wife, Carolyn, and I bought our house and moved back to Carnegie so I could work for the Kiowa tribe, I remember picking up the local newspaper and reading a list of all the burglaries, bad checks, and incidents of public drunkenness and the names of all the offenders. I hadn't seen such character assassination in a long time and was really offended by it. Now I thought how hard it was to live there, and I wanted to tell John how I felt about it but decided not to, not now, not perhaps for a while.

"I sat down and that's when I saw you and your boy," John Tofpi repeated. "Walking." He was leaving the text wide open again. He was, I think, allowing me to enter into his narrative and provide some of the answers myself. Like a stone tossed into a quiet pool, Kiowa narrative expands outward, ripple upon dark ripple, image upon image like the black waters in Homer's Odysseus story. Since I began work with the Kiowas I have noticed that many storytellers will open up a story and leave some parts of it unclear or unfinished so that the listener can provide some of the answers or comments or conclusions on his or her own. A huge section of the story may remain open for hours or days or even weeks (Sarris 1993). I learned that you could hear a story and go back to it days later when the storyteller would pick it up again and continue. I have had to remember where we had left off storytelling, the way you do when you lay down a novel you're reading and pick it up the following week and have to piece the story back together again in your mind. A lot of what John was doing, and not only in this instance, was giving me the opportunity to participate in his story. I could even add my own story. If I didn't provide anything, it was all right too. I was beginning to learn that some stories don't even require a resolution or closure. Kiowas leave much story content up in the air. So I thought I should let John know that I would rather that he, not I, finish it somehow. He must have known that I understood the context he had been pulling in around us, must have believed that because I was Kiowa I should know what was going on. He'd been framing his story with the details of his life all this time: who his relatives were, what went on around him, his own state of mind—everything Kiowa he could think of, and now he had a story frame set up in the middle of our conversation. He wanted to get back into the story proper so he could explain what was going on inside of him. I sensed that perhaps he had gotten to the climax of his story now. I thought I could actually feel the story develop into a full-blown entity ready to burst forth like water from a broken dam.

"You two were coming down the hill just like that. It was hot. I'm surprised you didn't see me, because I was sitting right there under that tree. Did you see me?"

"I know, fàbí," I said, trying to keep up with him. "I don't know why we didn't see you." In my mind's eye I could see him sitting below that tall cottonwood, his daddy longlegs stretching out in front of him. Close by, the creek. The water gurgling in the gnarled roots under the steaming foliage.

"Gyah! Y'all just walked by. You know, I was sitting there."

"Why didn't you call out to us?" I wanted more story, but he seemed to want me to put something in myself. I noticed he kept a close eye on me. He was coaxing me, leading me into the story web he had spun so carefully. I had had the same kind of experience with my own grandpa when he told stories, and with Cornelius Spottedhorse, my other storytelling consultant. Cornelius, however, wasn't as insistent as John. Unlike John, he didn't pressure me to draw any conclusions or add any comments to his stories. Many of the Kiowa stories in my study were like this. The storyteller at some point allowed me, the listener, to comment, even if it was to just respond hàu. There are ethnographies of Native American storytelling in which fieldworkers have observed and participated in this exact storytelling technique (Sarris 1989, 1993, Basso 1990, Hymes 1981, Tedlock 1983). Other works, especially earlier ones, lack dialogue and participation. Elsie Clews Parsons (1929), Alice Marriott (1945), and S. Wilbur Nye (1962) collected Kiowa stories and concentrated on only the text or oral story itself and little else. These stories were hardly commented upon then or now. They are fairly well translated texts. Parsons's *Kiowa Tales* (1929) is the only one with an introduction and some cursory comments about the Kiowa people, her informants, and the Kiowa community. Her comparisons of Kiowa and Pueblo story themes, action, and characters are still valid and useful. Scholars who have worked with Kiowa narratives more recently have suspected her of interpreting most of the stories from her own limited perspective, as was typical during her time. But the lack of Kiowa interpretation of Kiowa stories is a matter of serious concern today.

Chapter III

Active Participation in Oral Narratives

Over the years, too many translations of Native American oral stories have been rushed into publication. I don't believe anybody has the capacity to do justice to stories collected hurriedly, translated, and shipped off to the press, and such behavior does serious injury to the work as a whole. So far, among non-Indians, Maurice Boyd (1981, 1983) may be the only one who has tried to give a cultural and tribal context to Kiowa stories he has published. He spent considerably more time in Kiowa homes doing that work than Parsons, who stayed barely two months in Kiowa country. Wilbur Nye (1962) may be another who seems to have known something about how Kiowas told stories. In each case, every one of these ethnographers focused mostly on the narrative content alone. They made few attempts to venture into the souls of the people whose stories they published. I am a little suspicious of outsiders who collect Indian stories and then make claims without giving the Indians a chance to comment. What I have attempted, and hope I have succeeded to some degree in doing in this book, is to enter into storytelling as event, let the storyteller's voice and the story itself speak, as it were. I have tried to stand back yet to participate in the narrative event when the story-teller invited me. It was often hard for me to comment upon or make any interpretations of the story as it was being told. Participation made all the difference: to be both listener and participant makes Kiowa storytelling manifest and whole. Only when there is that twofold experience can the wonder and ceremony that is Kiowa storytelling occur. There are so many ways that Kiowas frame and contextualize storytelling that in-depth knowledge and understanding of the phenomenon will take years of study. It's a little early yet to know a lot about the storytelling genre of Kiowas. I believe there will be an understanding in time, and I believe that we will begin to recognize some very familiar storytelling features we didn't know were there.

"I don't know why I didn't call out to you," John continued, having left off in order to speak with an elder who had interrupted us. I'd gotten up and fetched him and me another cup of hot coffee. The steam rose from our styrofoam cups in billows big as mountains. We had entered an enchanted storyland by now and I was full of excitement. John was himself smiling quite a bit now. "I was just sitting there," he said in all seriousness. "It was broad daylight too. Sure it was."

Now I have my clue, I thought. He *was* there. His dream story is fused with something he actually went out to do. He had dreamed the tree and set out to locate it, down by the bridge by our house! I must ask him to be sure this is the case. I imagine he was in a prayerful state and didn't want to interrupt himself out there. Maybe that's why he didn't say anything to us. John Tofpi is complex. He sometimes doesn't want to say too much. He may protect himself that way. If he knows you aren't paying any attention to him, he's liable not to make his presence known. He's secretive that way, I believe. That day on the road, when Jeff and I had not noticed him, he may have wanted to be a spectator. He wasn't in any mood to talk, and maybe he didn't want a lot of questions asked either. Somebody might have laughed and said, "We saw old Slow down by a bridge sitting there." John T. would not take that chance. We didn't know what he was doing down there. If we did, we might have embarrassed him. People don't always take John seriously around there. He's always had to make people laugh and like him, I had heard someone remark once. They don't understand the real man under the clothes he is wearing, I think I'd responded, or they don't appreciate his true feelings.

After John finished talking about that episode down at the bridge and the strange apparition, he changed the subject quickly to his own relatives, and that's how the session ended. This day what he appeared to have done was leave the story open. The next time we talked, a few weeks later, he wanted to talk about how we were kin to each other. When I asked him about his dream story again, he just nodded his head, smiled, and said, "I dreamed it. Yeah. Sure I did."

I think I wanted facts this time. I wanted him to say in his own words that he had gone looking for that dream tree. I wanted to be sure how he told stories. He seemed to be storytelling the way my grandfather told stories, mixing dreams, fantasies, and facts. Fusing everything together, as it were. Making stories holistic. Whole. Proving a point. Everything coming together into one unified Kiowa reality. But John wouldn't let that happen. Not yet.

"You mean that tree thing you saw in your dream? You saw it and looked for that very tree?"

"I did," he replied. He took his hand and shaped it into the figure of a tree again. "It was shaped like this."

Two weeks had passed since we last talked, and it was as if the story had never concluded from the first telling. He was right in the midst of it again and going just as strong as ever. I was completely taken by this. Amazed.

"And that's what you saw down by the bridge where we live?" I pressed on.

He nodded his head vigorously, happy I remembered that detail. "Right there."

I had the whole answer now, I thought. I felt satisfied. Now I knew that when he reopened the story, if he ever did, I would have a different frame of reference from which to work. I made a note of that in my notebook. I figured that if he was going to tell me more dream stories there might be a chance that they could be partly dreams and partly real occurrences. It was hard to tell what might be real and what might not be unless I came right out and asked him.

A few days after our session I thought about John T.'s story. I remembered reading something Dennis Tedlock (1983) had written on the often dreamlike or fantastic things that go on in oral narratives. He had written to the effect that one did not need to "look to modern children's fairy tales, or to modern dreams, or to the concept of 'prelogical mentality' (which still survives, implicitly, in psychoanalytic attempts to treat tales as collective dreams)" to understand the fantastic features of oral narratives (p. 177). I could see that people who were not used to these kinds of stories could be easily confused by them. Consider for a moment all the bizarre happenings in the Bible. There are winged animals. Voices that speak out of the sky. Serpents that talk to and tempt people. There is portrayed a sort of magic kingdom where everything is beautiful and there is an aura of tranquillity and magic found nowhere in life. Imagine looking up in the sky and seeing a flaming vehicle with four sets of wheels that have eyes embedded all around the spokes. This last spectacle appeared in an account by a man considered holy in those days. The sighting is itself represented as something so miraculous that even the individual who witnessed it had trouble believing his eyes. The irony here is that many people read the story and are moved spiritually by it. I have to ask myself, Are readers affected by the object or the extraordinary account?

I read somewhere that what Ezekiel in fact saw was a UFO. In biblical times. Some UFO enthusiasts thought this was an excellent case of extraterrestrial contact. Many sought out accounts of like occurrences throughout the Bible. Others began searching elsewhere. Now we have people in astronomy, archaeology, physics, and just about every field of scientific endeavor puzzling over visitors from outer space.

I don't want to get too far away from Kiowa oral storytelling, but I need to take a little time to go out on the narrative limb, as it were. So I can clear up any misunderstanding people might have about oral storytelling, Kiowa oral storytelling. Was my good friend John Tofpi himself recounting a story that contained some aspects of the supernatural? What some literary theorists call magic realism?

My grandfather told me a good many stories that contained strange or otherwise unbelievable characters and incidents. One that comes to mind is the account of Táimê, with which I want to close this chapter. Táimê is the name of the sun dance medicine bundle. It is also the essence or spirit that surrounds the ritualistic dance itself. Some refer to T<u>a</u>imê as a deity, although I do not believe that they do so today. In any event, T<u>a</u>imê is said to have come to the Kiowas a long time ago when the tribe lived on the northern Plains. There are several versions of how it happened. The one I am familiar with is the one my grandfather told. His account contains many remarkable and unusual incidents. It is dream-like. But in the main it is a testimony of Kiowa faith and reveals, I believe, a good many insights into the spirituality of the Kiowa people, at least from my grandfather's perspective. It is also a good example of how important Kiowa values are passed down, which is one of the primary objectives of storytelling.

The Coming of T<u>a</u>imê to the Kiowas

Much of the truth that Zunis see in their fictional narratives, Tedlock points out, derives "from the efforts of the narrator to create the appearance of reality within the body of the story itself. The ability to create this appearance," he goes on, "is the most important measure of the individual narrator's skill" (p. 166).[1] My grandfather's skill was well developed. His long story about when T<u>a</u>imê came to the Kiowas illustrates just how skillfully he made fantastic things seem real. The recording of my grandfather telling the story was itself made in 1964 by John Chaddlesone, a Kiowa Methodist preacher, who at the time was pastor at Mount Scott Kiowa Methodist Church, Lawton, Oklahoma, and my grandfather's granddaughter's husband. The entire recording is in spoken Kiowa, a transcription of which I have included in the Appendix.

Imagine that you are a child hearing this story for the first time. Or better, become a child. Enter the story as you would an open door into a magical kingdom and be prepared to believe anything you hear.

The Coming of T<u>a</u>imê to the Kiowas

1   Long ago.
2   O, so long ago.
3   It must have been back when life first began.

4   Somewhere during that time a very poor young man there was.

5   Perhaps he was down and out.

6   Or perhaps he was without relatives but he was poor and he was taken in by a very old man and his very old wife.

7   But then he accommodated their food needs.

8   And now I am telling you the story exactly as I know it.

9   Although someone may know it better than I do, this is still going to be the best [story version] I know.

10   All right then, maybe he was down and out, as I said.

11   But then the old man and woman were hard pressed just to survive.

12   And then he went out one day to hunt and he must have taken a firearm or a bow and arrows. It is not clear what firearm he bore but he went hunting.

13   And then all at once he came upon a set of animal tracks and they were buffalo tracks.

14   A buffalo had laid down these tracks.

15   And it was probably hard times because during winter the buffalo usually grazed elsewhere and not here.

16   For some unknown reason here were tracks.

17   And so he followed the tracks.

18   Perhaps I will kill this one and take it home, he thought.

19   And he followed the tracks.

20   And he followed the tracks, when it occurred to him that the sun had set.

21   The sun lowered and it was dusk.

22   He thought: Now then, I'm going to let it go now and go home.

23   And come back tomorrow and maybe there will be tracks left.

24   And I shall again take up the search, he thought.

25   And so he went home.

26   And he arrived where they were camped.

27   And he slept.

28   In the morning after breakfast once more he went out.

29   And he arrived where he had left off his search the day before.

30   All right then, he followed where the tracks led.

31   And he tracked.

32   He tracked and sure enough the tracks were newly made.

33   And he was encouraged.

34   And then before he knew it was dusk.

35   And so he had to leave off there.

36   And he journeyed home.

37   And again he slept.

38   Early the next morning he sallied out and where he'd left off
      tracking he arrived and sure enough here were the tracks.

39   And so he followed the tracks that trailed fresh animal droppings.

40   Right here dirt had been stirred up in a pool of drinking water.

41   Clearly he was closing in and would find what he was looking for,
      he pondered, as he proceeded.

42   And now it was the third night.

43   Again it became dusk.

44   But then here lay tracks so fresh.

45   Heaped up right here were droppings.

46   And still steamy.

47   Ah! Night was growing up.

48   And so he left off and lay down to sleep.

49   The fourth time, it was the fourth time he'd gone out looking.

50   In the morning he left and here now and there and beyond lay a
      misty cloud.

51   And so, on the fourth day he encountered it.

52   He encountered it.

53   He encountered it.

54   He trailed the buffalo four days.

55   He found it.

56   He found it and it transformed into a man.

57   It transformed into a man.

58   And the man said, "Come here. Come here. Accompany me," he
      exclaimed.

59   And he went with the man.

60   Because he was probably afraid.

61   Perhaps he was entranced.

62   Who knows.

63   And so he went with the man and they came to a big mountain
      and the man led him inside the mountain.

64   And so the man led him inside the mountain.

65   And there he kept him a captive.

66   And it was there that he began to teach him.

67   And so it was that he taught him things.

68   This sun dance, as they call it, and the dancing was what he taught him.

69   It was ritual prayer.

70   It was ritual prayer.

71   That was what he was teaching him.

72   And so it was that what he taught him he learned.

73   And so he asked him to exit and he went outside and left.

74   And he arrived at home.

75   He arrived at home.

76   And so it happened that this old man and this old woman were no longer human beings anymore.

77   And so he told them, "All right now, I have stayed with you a long time.

78   I have remained a long time," he said.

79   "I must go now," he said.

80   And so this old man—he and his wife were seated together—he said, "there are two things tied up in bundles and suspended on a rack inside the tipi," he said. "Go see for yourself."

81   "See for yourself," he repeated.

82   "Because you have treated us well and lived with us."

83   "You have provided for us and so go look at it."

84   "I will give you one or the other," he said.

85   "I shall give you one of them."

86   And this is what he said.

87   Now which one was it?

88   One might have been yellow and the other might have been blue.

89   Now which one was it exactly?

90   But there were two of them.

91   And so he took one of them which turned out to be ritual prayer custom or tradition, now the ritual sun dance lodge, as it is told.

92   The sun dance.

93   *You understand the term* Táimê?

94   Sun dance lodge.

95   That was apparently the ritual prayer.

96   It was apparently the summer prayer.

97   *Do you understand clearly now?*

98   It was apparently the summer prayer ceremony.

99   Alongside life as it evolves.

100   In the summertime when every living thing ripens and becomes conscious.

101   Rain dampens the earth.

102   Everything is wet and the grass grows lush.

103   Flowers!

104   Every kind of fruit imaginable grows is what it was.

105   And so this was summer.

106   Summertime.

107   The fullness of deep summer.

108   Creation itself.

109   Apparently in the summertime everything becomes conscious and [that is] why it can ripen.

110   It was food and it was life.

111   LIFE.

112   It was prayer ritual that he had apparently taken hold of and made his own.

113   Táimê is what they call it.

114   The sun dance is what it is.

115   It is the summer prayer ritual.

116   In the middle of summer when all the fruit ripens.

117   During August, during September.

118   Around this time everything ripens.

119   All fruits!

120   Fruit.

121   It was every kind of food you eat.

122   It was everything that grows on this earth and it was the prayer ritual, everything that Táimê was in charge of. It was all of this.

123   They say it is the prayer tradition of Táimê that everybody cried out ecstatically in one voice.

124   Everybody was overjoyed.

125   It would occur every summer during this time.

126   Apparently this is where they pitched their prayers.

127   They initiated their prayers and went forth.

128 And it was during this time they came together.

129 It was during this gathering that the buffalo grazed nearby.

130 With abundant ripe food.

131 These foods. All the kinds when they ripen.

132 Right in the middle of the ripening season, it was.

133 All foods, there were.

134 All right, right in the middle of the ripening of foods they prepared themselves and this is where they made their prayer.

135 They prayed the sun dance.

136 It was during this big prayer that everybody came together and camped.

137 And the prayer they made right there.

138 Apparently they were giving thanks to God.

139 They were praying in thanksgiving.

140 This here sun dance it was.

141 It was at this Kiowa prayer-making where the Kiowas were of one accord.

142 And it was the Kiowa prayer tradition.

143 It was the Kiowa prayer tradition right there.

144 The sun dance was the Summer prayer ceremony.

145 He [Táimê] was in charge of the ritual.

146 *Do you understand the meaning clearly now?*

147 Now then, the Kiowas prayed through the Ten Medicine Bundles.

148 Them.

149 He was the keeper of the prayer.

150 This prayer way was given to the Kiowas in the beginning.

151 Words. The Kiowa language and these things, these Kiowa ten medicine bundles, they say, those.

152 And prayer.

153 With them [ten medicine bundles] the Kiowas could pray.

154 It is for the future.

155 It was religion.

156 *Is that what you call prayer?*

157 The Kiowas made the big prayer first during the sun dance, and everything else.

158 The feast also.

159 And the buffalo themselves.

160 Everything came together at this time.

161 And everybody played and had a good time when it came together.

162 They were praying.

163 It was a big prayer.

164 They wanted to always come together in the summertime.

165 Very old women.

166 Ancient ones.

167 Real old.

168 They prayed for these too.

169 Children. He-yo-he! O-yo-he-yo! He-yo-he! He-yo-ho!

170 Them.

171 They prayed for the children.

172 All right, everyone.

173 It was for the Kiowas and for every Kiowa society.

174 Right there, everybody was praying.

175 And they were dancing.

176 They were happy.

177 For four days.

178 Because everything is done in four days.

179 They prayed and danced for four days.

180 They were praying.

181 There in the middle of the sun dance lodge, without eating food and drinking water, the old ones prayed.

182 For life.

183 Right here on this earth.

184 Their humanity and the way they live their life.

185 It was the prayer tradition.

186 Every kind of dance was there.

187 Everything came together there.

188 Freedom and even carelessness and abandonment were there.

189 Nothing in life was barred.

190 It was the big Kiowa prayer.

191 Now, take a close look at it.

192 Right now, everything that you are asking about, including the dance tradition itself, you are doing to this very day.

193 The way you are dancing—because you wanted to know about the way we dance—it was all about the big prayer.

194   Now you know that the white man came ashore (and he is ruthless) and does things in an arrogant way.

195   He shattered it!

196   They annihilated The Beginning.

197   How ruthless!

198   Now take close look at it.

199   Now then, the last sun dance—The-Time-the-Buffalo-Hide-Hung sun dance, they call it—was the last such ceremony.

200   That one.

201   That one.

202   Apparently it was during the afternoon of that last sun dance when it happened.

203   It was then that everybody in the encampment saw it.

204   "There! Something is coming out! Something there!"

205   Everybody was in the camp when they saw it.

206   Right there in the middle of the sun dance lodge something white emerged.

207   And it grew larger and larger and they were all looking at it and it came out and got up and they were looking at it and it rose into the heavens, right there at the sacred sun dance, because that is where the Kiowas pray and why they are dancing.

208   That is where the dance first came that you wanted to know about and so I'm telling you.

209   So it is. That is all there is to say now.

To most people, unless they're Kiowa, this story is going to seem a fantasy or tall tale. There are just too many fantastic things going on in it. But to me and other Kiowas everything that happens and everything in the story are real. There is nothing in the Táimê story to which we cannot relate. I've talked to many Kiowas concerning these aspects of tribal tales and myths and legends, and all largely agree that the stories reflect how things actually were.

The story of Táimê is a magical story that seems to get longer at each telling. I have heard several versions of it. It falls in the category of traditional Kiowa stories but is not itself an origin myth. It could easily be identified as a fantastic story too. In the final analysis, I believe it is a traditional story because of the language and antiquity of it. It tells of how a young man came to understand the power of T<u>a</u>imê. It also tells of how, through an extraordinary encounter, T<u>a</u>imê came to be with the Kiowas and stayed perhaps for centuries. Many stories tell of encounters such as this one. How many stories I have heard that are similar! It seems every medicine man met up with some animal or bird or strange beast to learn from it how to effect magical cures and so forth. This kind of sacred knowledge was kept by the person, who either passed on the power to another member of the family or died. The sacred knowledge was kept in story form so it could be recounted just as the coming of T<u>a</u>imé was. Sadly, many of these stories are no longer told or have been forgotten altogether.

Leaving Stories Wide Open

With John Tofpi and other Kiowa storytellers, I learned to keep the narrative event and setting open so we could engage in a dialogic exchange at all times. John left much for me to fill in for myself, as I have said. In regard to verisimilitude, I could ask myself if what I heard was real or not. I could dwell on these kinds of questions if I wanted to. That was part of the idea perhaps. That was how some of the stories, including my own grandfather's, came. I had to tell myself this was one way Kiowas used to tell stories and perhaps how they still do. I was glad we were getting somewhere with how Kiowas told stories as time went along.

Yes, John left much of the story open for me to fill in myself. My appreciation and understanding were limited only by my own ability to believe or not believe, to hear and see both real and not real. In the final analysis, it probably didn't matter. I think he just provided a way for us to be closer as Kiowa kinsmen, whether I understood or not. His was in large measure a Kiowa gesture, what my mother deemed "the right Kiowa thing to do." All during my work with him and other Kiowa consultants there were occasions when this kinship bonding occurred. It was part ritual, part casual. The fact of the matter is I felt more and more Kiowa each time I met with one of my consultants, and we all developed a very close relationship during those months. I was glad that I had gotten close to my own parents, my Uncle Oscar Tsoodle, John Tofpi, Cornelius Spotted-horse, and the others.

When we finished talking this day, John got to his feet slowly. He was prepared to go home. He smiled. "Okay. Hey, guy, come back again real soon," he said and laughed. "We can talk some more. What do you say? I'll tell you about that good cedar and sage."

He'd been telling me a lot about *qólgá* or àu:hį̀: and séó:gá, the special plants used in Kiowa ritual. It was before he took me to cut them, and he was eager that I should know everything he cared about. These two plants defined him most clearly, I was to learn. This is how he wanted me to know him, but now he was ready to call it a day.

"My brother," I said in Kiowa. "I'm glad you were able to talk to me about those stories today."

We were both standing now. I felt rather lightheaded after our long ordeal that day. The Elders Center was quiet once more, as it had been earlier. It was late afternoon. The wind had died down outside. The sun, a bloody ball in the western sky, sank slowly to the dark earth, filling it with a deep silence. An unimaginable loneliness pervaded the land everywhere.

"Sure," said John Tofpi in a serious tone of voice. "I know lots of stories. We'll talk some more next time. You come again. We'll go out and cut some cedar. I know where it grows plentiful. It's good, that. Smells good. It's good."

He paused and looked up and around. "Hey, where's everybody?"

"What?"

"Where did all them old folks go?"

I looked around. There was nobody in the building.

"That's all right, guy," he laughed. "I guess they had to go home, ain't it?"

"You located a good place, didn't you? That cedar."

"I sure did. It's easy to get to. There's three places I cut cedar. Nobody knows. Just me I know. I can show you over there. Missouri Red. That's what them White folks call it. Must be some kind of science name, you know. Maybe so." He arched his eyebrows to let me know how important his findings were, that there was nothing better than knowing a secret and cherishing what it really was. "It's the best àu:hí: around though."

I walked him over to the front door. He held his crumpled cap in hand. My good friend John Tofpi was ready to open the door and depart. I looked down at his cap. It had a red-and-white Co-Op patch sewed across the front of it. I'd seen dozens just like it around Carnegie.

I gestured with my head toward the south. "It's not anywhere near Longhorn Mountain, is it?"

Longhorn Mountain is the site where Kiowas historically cut cedar. Every Kiowa who smoked cedar knew it. Asking him about Longhorn reminded me of Keith Basso's work on storytelling and place-names. Basso (1990) explains that social bonding occurs in Western Apache storytelling. He notes that the storytellers were often reinforcing tribal values and moral behavior. For instance, when an Apache wanted to teach his listener a lesson, he'd tell a place-name story. He wouldn't necessarily tell the entire story. Just mentioning the place-name was enough for the listener to remember what had taken place at that precise location. The Apaches told Basso that, for instance, if a man misbehaved while he was passing by some geographical region of the country and paid dearly, that incident and location were memorialized in a story. If a person misbehaved in the same way later, an Apache storyteller could simply make reference to the location and instantly the offender would recognize his error and mend his ways. Thus did Western Apaches conduct their lives as a unified people. I thought John Tofpi was a lot like those Apaches. He knew the importance of place-names and everything important that was associated with places. Perhaps there was some underlying meaning in Kiowa places and place-names too. I thought maybe I could ask him more about this next time.

"No," answered John. "It's somewhere else different. You'll see. I'll show you. Missouri Red."

He slipped his cap onto his head. Just before he started out the double doors, he hesitated, turned around. "Hey, little brother," he said, "that old man Tainpeah was my own grandpa. You know that?"

Tainpeah, my grandfather's oldest brother, died at an early age.[2] He was said to be the handsomest Kiowa alive in his time, and everybody in the Tenadooah family told only good things about him. He'd also married one of the most beautiful Kiowa women in the tribe, my grandmother's own sister.

"I know," I said. "We're related that close."

"You bet." He stepped out the door and disappeared into the dusk.

I left John Tofpi that day thinking about the cedar and sage. I thought about the places he mentioned where he cut the ceremonial plants. It reminded me of the moral significance that Apache storytellers put into their place-name stories. I thought how thoughtful he had been about my feelings about our kinship, how he had wanted me to know exactly where he and I stood as family and tribal members. For him, this was the honest Kiowa way of doing things. Like a Western Apache, he had learned how to conduct himself in the appropriate way. He was fulfilling his obligation as a Kiowa to be the best kind of man he could be. The Western Apaches did this in their place-name stories, and John T. did it by establishing his Kiowa relationship to me. I am sure he would have done the same for any other of his Kiowa relations if the occasion had presented itself. Every visit I made following this one in some way clarified Kiowa storytelling, the meaning of being Kiowa, and what being Kiowa meant to Kiowas and to me. I learned once and for all that what John Tofpi wanted most to do was establish our roles as kinsmen. Simple as that. This was his Kiowa obligation. Each time we met he made sure I understood how closely we were related.[3] Once we got that business out of the way we could talk about anything we wanted or tell a good Kiowa yarn.

Chapter IV

Knowing How and When to Tell a Story

Origin myths are among the oldest stories Kiowas tell. They compose what might be called classical Kiowa oral literature. Every Kiowa speaker knows one or more and can still recount some, though many have been forgotten because spoken Kiowa is in decline. Where once the old stories were told in Kiowa, nowadays many if not most are recounted in English. The Kiowas who told stories the old way were of an earlier generation: my grandfather, his brothers, sisters, and cousins. In my grandparents' home, many relatives came to visit. They spoke Kiowa fluently. For them, words came easily, as did the accompanying mannerisms that distinguished them as Kiowas. They could of course speak English, but it was spoken Kiowa that they used among themselves.

Part of the skill of telling Kiowa stories is preparation: to know when and how to tell stories. To sit on the edge of conversation until something suggests a story. Thus, a story will seemingly pop up out of nowhere. This ability to tell stories without warning is something I often observed while doing fieldwork. I have to admit that even though I grew up hearing Kiowas tell stories, I had not paid much attention to how it happened. As time went along, however, I began to notice that Kiowas were indeed talking and narrating stories at almost the same time. At first, it seemed ordinary enough. I'd seen non-Indian English speakers do the same thing. When people talk to one another they will often incorporate personal anecdotes, funny sayings, or asides into their conversation as added information or sometimes for the sheer pleasure of it. Most of us know people who do it skillfully, and perhaps we do it ourselves. It not only enlivens our speech but adds buoyancy and spontaneity, providing speakers and listeners alike a real joy. Kiowas knew how to tell stories this way because they had heard other Kiowas do it. They had listened to how other Kiowas told stories and mastered the skills themselves. In time, they began to use less Kiowa and more English. When I was a boy, most storytelling was in Kiowa. These days, however, Kiowas tell stories in English, but they make you laugh anyway.

A Kiowa Trickster

One cannot talk about Kiowa storytelling without mentioning the trickster, Séndé. Séndé, or Saynday, is in some ways the equivalent of the Greek god Hermes. Paul Radin (1969), perhaps the best-known trickster scholar, notes that the "overwhelming majority of all so-called trickster myths in North America give an account of the creator of the earth, or at least the transforming of the world, and have a hero who is always wandering, who is always hungry, who is not guided by normal conceptions of good or evil, who is either playing tricks on people or having them played on him and who is highly sexed" (p. 155). Radin writes that the "two-fold function of benefactor and buffoon . . . is the outstanding characteristic of the overwhelming majority of trickster heroes wherever they are encountered in aboriginal America" (p. 124).

Alice Marriott (1947), who has written extensively about the Kiowas and Kiowa folklore, gives an account of Séndé: "Kiowa Indian people believe and tell about how things got started and came to be." She contends,

Saynday was the one, they say, who got lots of things in our world started and going. Some of them were good, and some of them were bad, but all of them were things that make the world the way it is.

Saynday is gone now. He lived a long time ago, and all these things happened a long way back. When he was here on the earth, he was a funny-looking man. He was tall and thin, and he had a little thin mustache that drooped down over his mouth. The muscles of his arms and legs bulged out big and then pulled in tight, as if somebody had tied strings around them. He had a funny, high, whiny voice, and he talked his own language. His language was enough like other people's so they could understand it, but it was his own way of talking, too.

Because Saynday got things started in the world, he could make the rules for the way these stories were going to be told. These are the rules that Saynday made, and if you didn't keep them he could cut off your nose: Always tell my stories in the winter, when the outdoors work is finished. (p. 7)

I don't think any Kiowas were ever harmed by telling a Séndé story before it got dark or in a season other than winter, at least not recently. I'm sure Kiowas did and perhaps still do break the storytelling rules. Probably nobody has ever bothered to look around to see if there are any clues that such violations and their repercussions have occurred. I can imagine the newspaper headlines if indeed they had. Flash: Local Kiowa Gets Nose Hacked Off for Telling Séndé Stories Wrong Time of Day.

I think the Séndé tales belong to the best comic literature in this country. First of all, they meet the requirement to inform or entertain or both. Next, they are creations in a language unlike any known. By this, I mean they are irrevocably original and American, and therefore cultural gems in their own right. The Séndé stories and all indigenous literatures, for that matter, sprang from and have developed in the American landscape since time immemorial. They are truly American, which leads us to the next question.

What Constitutes "Indian Literature"?

Who determines what is serious literature? Western readers cannot easily appreciate Indian texts per se (Blaeser 1970, Sarris 1993). They have been trained to read only certain kinds of texts regarded as "literature." What Americans learn in school is that there are certain kinds of writing that are literature. We are given books that contain these writings, and we grow up learning that this is what real literature is. Anything else is not literature by definition (Ong 1982). We are also given lists of so-called serious literature that includes works by American writers such as Emerson, Whitman, Melville, Faulkner, Hemingway, Steinbeck, Fitzgerald, and Poe, to name a few. In modern times the list has grown to include works by N. Scott Momaday, Louise Erdrich, James Welch, and other American Indian authors. But when we consider people we know who tell stories or recite long narratives that have been translated into English, we suddenly realize there is something wrong. Our list contains people who often cannot speak the English language well, much less write it. Many of these storytellers have little or no formal education but tell stories in a traditional Indian way. Furthermore, nobody outside their culture seems to listen to their stories or understand what they may have to offer.

When we Indians hear the stories our own people tell, they are just as funny and informative as Faulkner's and Twain's are for English readers. Our stories include all kinds of characters. They speak, harangue, cheat, steal, fight, fall in love, die. They say funny things in interesting ways. There is a plot in our stories. And action. Sometimes. But none of these stories has been included in the canon of American literature. Maybe it is because many have not been translated and written down. It is difficult to find any examples of indigenous or minority literatures included in any respectable or serious literary collection. Stories by Native Americans usually end up in an anthology devoted to "Native American literature." I do not mean contemporary writers like Louise Erdrich, Scott Momaday, or James Welch. I am referring to traditional and contemporary Indian storytellers, who speak their native languages and tell stories their own tribal way.

Indian Literature Is . . .

At a regional symposium on Indian literature some time back, Kimberly Blaeser discussed the existing body of American Indian writing in America. One of her main concerns, a concern shared by many who are interested in Indian literature, was What exactly constitutes Indian literature? Does it have to be written? Or can it be oral? Either way, does the writer or storyteller have to be Indian? Or does the text only have to deal with Indian subject matter or be populated by Indians and have an Indian theme?

A few years later the same sort of questions arose regarding Indian art. Apparently, artists painting Indians and Indian subject matter were passing themselves off as Indian artists though they belonged to no Indian tribe. Artists who were enrolled members of a tribe were incensed. This controversy led art galleries to start scrutinizing all the Indian art shows they hosted to make sure that artists who claimed to be Indian had documents to prove their genuineness.

It is easy to see how confusing these issues of authenticity in the arts and literature can be. In Indian literature, the question always arises whether one is an Indian or non-Indian writing literature about Indians and Indian life. The crux of the matter, about the same as the one in the arts, is that what is Indian literature to some is not necessarily Indian literature to others. (So the argument goes.) My point is: Indians and other well-meaning folks interested in Indians have the right to question authenticity, but we do not always know exactly how we are to proceed to define and determine it.

For me, it is easy to see what constitutes oral Indian literature because it insists on the use of spoken native language. To locate literature that is oral, one need only go out into the field with recorder in hand and collect examples in the original language. These recordings would then be transcribed in a writing system that is comprehensible to someone who wants to examine the content. The question of authenticity is nil. This, in my opinion, is oral Indian literature.

Everything else aside, what I have been trying to do here is show how much easier it is to define what is Indian literature when it is spoken than when it is written. Defining written Indian literature, like identifying authentic Indian art, has always been a tenuous undertaking and will perhaps be for a long time.

The same kind of questions can be raised regarding translation. Can Native American literary oral art be translated so that it meets the expectations of intelligent readers? What is the best way to do this? If we confront something literary, on whose aesthetic principles are we going to stand? When I started collecting and transcribing Kiowa stories, I had little trouble. The difficulties began when I started to translate the Kiowa into English. First of all, it was hard to find corresponding words. Then there was the problem of making sense out of things that didn't require exact words but relied upon inferences that required explanation. For instance, when Kiowas say "Séndé áhêl" (Séndé came along), two Kiowa words convey the hearsay or storytelling mode. But the translator, in order to convey both the meaning and the mode, has to add something: Séndé *reportedly* came along; without the adverb, the verb does not sound Kiowa and does not suggest the storyteller's role. If you make a point or develop a kind of dramatic ending to Kiowa stories, as you do with stories written in English, they will seem unnatural, at least to Kiowas. It's always safest to make an almost word-for-word translation so the English reader can get some sense of the meaning in the stories.

Kiowa stories occur anytime in the midst of ordinary conversation. There is no special preparation for telling a story. The listener has to be ready for it. You have to "just listen pretty close and you can hear a story," John Tofpi later told me. He said that stories "kind of happen." But that was about a year after I'd visited with my Uncle Oscar Tsoodle at my mother's home, after Oscar had died. I am sure I will not be hearing anything quite as beautiful as the conversations and stories we recorded together. And I believe he knew our visit would be the last time he would say what he needed to say: Why my dear Kiowa uncle told me he was going to tell me that one story that hot day right at the end of our visit, in 1998, at my mother's home. He might have been prepared to tell me this one story a long time before that day. Maybe he had decided to wait. Perhaps he thought that we should exhaust everything we needed to before he opened that beautiful story I could show off to my friends and colleagues. I have referred to it time and time again, because it is so fascinating, and so Kiowa. I'd heard such stories as a boy. The tone of his voice rang with true Kiowa knowing and authority. When he uttered the words I came immediately into the presence of that long ago time, far out on the prairie where Kiowas lived. I knew as soon as he told the story that I must journey with him in my imagination to a very special place. I somehow instinctively knew that I should never hear a story like this again.

This story or "telling" was actually a story within a story, told to him long ago by his old grandfather Tenadooah. I am not sure how it was framed in the original. Perhaps other tales or even singing had preceded and followed it once. It could have been a story invoked by some special signs like a recital of charms. Perhaps it was just told right out in the middle of everyday conversation like any oral narrative.

1   He said the Kiowas were camping.
2   He said that.
3   They built a human corral, he said.
4   That's the way they used to kill deer around here.
5   They must have chased them thereabouts.
6   And then they chased them this way [toward the human corral].
7   The deer were exhausted.
8   Suddenly one of the deer began to sing, grandpa said.
9   The deer sang, he said.
10   And he said they ran it just right along there.
11   And then they chased it this way, he said.

Uncle Oscar paused right here. He left the story hanging in the air between us, suspended in space, as it were. When he looked at me again, an expression of serious intent had set like an enormous bright light upon his face. He smiled. "You know we always tell stories this way because of our children," he said.

I nodded my head in agreement. Yes. The story was still open. Nothing seemed amiss. The Kiowa custom was to stop the telling and wait for somebody to make a remark, interject something. I imagine he wanted me to say what I felt about the singing or make a direct response to his statement about children. In the Kiowa way, he wanted to be absolutely sure that I was getting the main point of his story. Throughout the afternoon he and my father had been talking back and forth, one telling a lengthy story and pausing occasionally so the other could respond. They were constantly opening up the conversation for impromptu storytelling. They rarely asked questions of each other or anybody else around the table where the four of us—my father, my mother, Uncle Oscar, and I—were seated. One or another of us made comments, some short, others long, another complex. Then whoever was talking at the time would go on. Many times one of us interjected what seemed totally unrelated, a remark about someone, usually a relative, or "prior texts," as William Foley (1997) called past anecdotes or narratives that keep showing up in newer contexts, what M. Bakhtin (1981) called "intertextualizations."[1]

In any event, Uncle Oscar was telling me what he thought was going on in the story at this point. He presented to me its main themes, particularly the survival of the Kiowa generations, noting that even animals are aware of their place in the world and their continuity as a species and that without this knowledge there is no purpose to living and life. A man or animal may live but a short space on earth. When a man or animal accomplishes a special purpose or renders some special service to other living beings in the short span of his life, then it is a well-spent life. This is what he was trying to get at as he told the story, or at least I thought this was what he was doing. His commentary was so skillfully interjected that it formed an understandable and natural part of the story. Later I thought this hiatus for his asides was really central to the story as a whole. That is, the commentary mattered in a significant way. The story was dependent upon it perhaps, and not the other way around. The story may have been just a vehicle. I don't know for sure.

I wished I had asked him more about that. I know he would have talked for hours. He was just that kind of a storyteller. A true Kiowa storyteller, he would have elaborated on it and would have told me how great life is, that we humans are not only lucky to be alive, but that we, the animals, and all living things serve some important, useful end, though we know not what. I thought, no wonder animals could speak Kiowa long ago. How could they not? No wonder Kiowas could make buffalo, eagles, bears, lizards, snapping turtles, waterbirds, and swift hawks special partners in this life and did not consider them just material for clothing or dwellings or food. Animals could impart powers to doctor and heal. I know this because my grandfather was himself a doctor. The magpie and waterbird helped him, and all of us whom he had treated at one time or another owed so much to the existence of these worldly creatures. We recovered from the trauma of serious illnesses and lived because my grandfather doctored us with the aid of another species of living creature.

"You know we always tell stories this way," Uncle Oscar picked up his deer story again. "Because of our children."

12	You tell stories for the sake of your children.
13	The deer sang, he said.
14	I heard it.
15	They were delivering the deer right up here, he said.
16	And so here it came, the Mother deer cantering along, he said.
17	And it was singing! He said.
18	And it sang:
19	He-ye-ya! He-ye-ya! He-ye-ya!
20	He-ye-yo! He-ye-ye-ye!
21	Here it approached, he said.
22	And the deer's tongue was hanging out of its mouth, he said.
23	And its child followed behind it.
24	And then she uttered song words, he said.
25	Hey! You all listen!
26	Listen up!
27	Right along there it was coming along. Singing!
28	Right along here it is singing! He said.
29	He-yeya! He-ye-ya! He-ye-ya!
30	He-ye-yo! He-ye-ye-ye!
31	Would that I had died instead!
32	I lament!
33	I lament that my child is going to die now!
34	This is my song!
35	He-ye-ye-ye!
36	The Mother deer sang, he said.
37	And I was there and heard it.

Chapter IV ◎ Knowing How and When to Tell a Story

In his long study of oral narratives, Richard Bauman (1977) has written that everything that surrounds narratives, all framing, including performance, "is accomplished through the employment of culturally conventionalized metacommunication. In empirical terms, this means that each speech community will make use of a structured set of distinctive communicative means from among its resources in culturally conventionalized and culture-specific ways to key the performance frame, such that all communication that takes place within that frame is to be understood as performance within that community" (p. 16). What Bauman means is that no matter how hard we resist we cannot escape the social or cultural milieu in which our stories occur. Every time we tell a tale or recount a fable, somehow or another we have to convey a sense of the community, people, and values around us. If I am to believe this to be true and apply it to Kiowa storytelling, then I have to imagine the old man Tenadooah when he tells his deer story. There are certain narrative frames he has to provide his listeners in order for them to understand his tale. A traditional Kiowa listener is obviously aware of the special close relationship of animals and men. For a traditional Kiowa, there will be no need to explain how a deer can speak directly to a man, for indeed it is in the nature of things that this can happen. Old man Tenadooah, for example, told of the time he lay on top of Mount Sheridan and of how, as he lay praying, a collared lizard, sometimes called a mountain boomer, big as a greyhound, confronted him, barking, trying to make him go away. When he recounted this event, there was no question but that it was a real occurrence, and his Kiowa listeners could not but believe him, as they should. And that is how the context of place and things and human values works its way into narratives, and what I believe Bauman and others in the field to be talking about.

Storytelling Collaboration

Let me just reiterate that Kiowas tell stories within stories. They construct a kind of metanarration. They make commentaries about the story during storytelling or afterwards. They talk about the content sometimes, account for it, so to speak. For example, when Uncle Oscar finished telling the mother deer story he came back to the theme of survival and talked about life being worthwhile, about living a long life in the right way, about the goal of life being to serve some special purpose. Sometimes Kiowas take a story from the past, a myth or legend, and leap with it into the midst of a new story.

Finally, Kiowas reflect on ideas, themes, and action that someone else may have concocted perhaps some time ago. The story the old man Tenadooah told Uncle Oscar, Uncle Oscar then retold to me. He took a "prior text" and put it into a new context. It came out of someone else's experience down through the years to right now.

The song the mother deer sang is a song of sorrow. The song is plaintive and beautiful. What is striking about the whole story is that it talks about the encounter between man and a sentient animal. This is no ordinary encounter. This is no ordinary animal. There is something different and almost human about that mother deer. She has an imploring tone.

I believe that the story inspires feelings of hope and compassion in the people. One of the stories my grandfather tells is about his own father's story about climbing Mount Sheridan to pray and being thrown off four times to the ground before his prayer was finally answered. That is also what a Western listener might regard as a fantastic tale. The uninitiated don't know how to take these kinds of stories. They don't understand what's going on in the Kiowa mind. In other words, who would believe a deer can talk to a man? And if this wasn't enough, sing a song to the hunters, the ones who would kill the deer without remorse? If someone other than a Kiowa hears this story, he or she might explain it away as a dream. Or as a tall tale.

In the final analysis it may not even matter if people believe in somebody else's stories. But the kinds of things that happen in Kiowa stories are, for Kiowas, real events and not supernatural ones, no matter what anybody says. Kiowas tell stories and the events in stories as if they know that they happened, and that's the way many of those stories have come down to us. When heard or read, they have to be taken on their own terms. One must enter the narrative as a child would enter an enchanted forest. That is the only way to understand and enjoy these stories. By and large, stories, all stories, have to be taken for their own sake or they would not even be stories. Preconceived notions about storytelling and stories will only lead to frustration and disappointment. The Kiowa stories are fascinating but require the listener to do more than simply listen to the text itself. They will require a good ear to listen with and participation of the whole and conscious being of the person.

And finally, old Kiowa stories constitute the best ideas Kiowas have of themselves. They are acts of the imagination and memory. They tell of time immemorial. By means of these stories Kiowas are able to remember people and relive events important in tribal history and culture. Indeed, the miracle of those noble and heroic times is evoked and comes alive in the imaginations and minds of Kiowas every time the old stories are told. Scott Momaday (1970), perhaps the best spokesman and advocate for oral traditions, has written that "the oral tradition is that process by which the myths, legends, tales, and lore of a people are formulated, communicated, and preserved in language by word of mouth, as opposed to writing" (p. 56). I should like to think that the process of telling stories continues today, that people, the Kiowas in particular, still formulate a tradition of narrations even as they have in the past.

When I set out to learn about Kiowa storytelling I approached it through translated texts. These were oral renderings transcribed into Kiowa and then translated into English. They were done well by Parker McKenzie and others. They included the nuances and special language features that I had always regarded as necessary in storytelling. Nothing seemed amiss here. Everything seemed to be in its place, including the famous formulaic openings and closings I had heard in stories as a child. I had spent a good many years writing my own stories in English and thought I had a good grasp on literature. It seemed likely to me that some of the same things I had studied in literature and then wrote about were a part of any language group or literary tradition. But when I started to examine the oral narratives as they were being spoken and recorded in Kiowa, I realized that something quite apart from traditional literature was going on. The people who were recounting the stories did so naturally, without formal training in the craft, without having enrolled in a course on storytelling. Like the storytellers of old they told stories as they had heard others tell them. More than likely they observed and learned storytelling technique from their grandparents. I do not mean to imply that only grandparents told stories. Indeed, there are storytellers in all age groups. In Kiowa culture, however, it has always been the almost exclusive right of a grandparent to pass along tradition. This includes storytelling. Every Kiowa grandparent was and still is a potential storyteller.

While I was recording in the field, no one came along and said so-and-so is a storyteller. When I asked, Who tells stories? or Who is a storyteller? I might as well have asked who the man in the moon was. No Kiowa volunteered any names. All Kiowas tell stories. Scott Momaday has written superb stories and novels. Momaday, who is a poet and winner of a Pulitzer Prize in fiction, writes exclusively in English. He is Kiowa but does not speak the Kiowa language. He has been asked to make public appearances all over the world, and people naturally assume he is a storyteller, which he is, though not in the Kiowa sense, not insofar as the term applies to the oral Kiowa world.

Cultural Aspects and Values in Storytelling

Richard Bauman (1977) notes that performance as a mode of spoken communication consists "in the assumption of responsibility to an audience for a display of communicative competence" (p. 16). He means that the speaker or storyteller must display a certain degree of social competence in order for his hearers to follow. The Kiowa story, if told properly, must include the stuff cultures are made of and that make up the tribal domain. Sometimes referred to as the context of the story, the social values that make up the themes in stories are those things that are meaningful to the people. If a story contains acts of heroism and bravery, it is because those are the values that are important to the people who will hear the stories. If generosity and closeness of family are important, these are the attributes that the storyteller invokes when recounting a story. In other words, stories are embedded in the social and cultural fiber of people or the tribe. Without these features no story can be told. Stories are by their nature framed by the social context.

Narrative Frameworks

Along these same lines I would like to say that storytelling cannot occur without story frames or devices to separate it from normal conversation. This notion of performance as a frame is the means by which we contrast literal communication from a more aesthetic one. When people joke, quote, translate, orate, dramatize, or do interpretive speeches, they generally provide some kind of performative frame to distinguish what they are doing from ordinary speech. By means of such devices as formulaic openings, the listeners are more readily tuned in to what is being said and respond accordingly. What comes before and what comes after speech is as important as how one responds to it. Without story-framing features, talk is simply talk. For the Kiowas, a performative mode requires that storytellers and listeners know the appropriate way stories are told and the appropriate response. The performative mode gives rise to a methodology for storytelling that over time developed into a fine art. Since stories are told and not written, the people who engage in telling stories or listening to them have to remember everything in the story text as well as the story context. Although there are no formally taught methods or techniques for storytelling, Kiowa storytellers seem to evolve naturally, and some of them become great.

At one time every Kiowa child knew how the Kiowas first came into this world or how Séndé and the animals stole the sun from the strangers far to the east. Every tender Kiowa ear could distinguish the sounds those faraway creatures made as they played with the sun, as they tossed that fiery orb back and forth and jeered at anybody who dared to approach. I can imagine that long-ago Kiowa camp. This is no tiny mountain village where the inhabitants sing merrily all day and laugh and dance. No. It is a foreboding place filled with misery. Darkness, like a substance, pervades everything. Giants walk among men striking fear into the hearts of the people who groan out in agony, "When will our deliverance come? When will there be light?" They pray for relief that will not come.

When I asked several of my storytelling consultants if they remembered the story, several of them said they did. Although there were as many different versions as there were those who had heard, they had marveled at it just as I had. By and large, the story had remained intact down through the ages.

"Did you ever receive any formal instruction on how to tell the old stories?" I always asked and was always told no. "Then how could you remember the old story?"

They didn't know. These Kiowa storytellers had learned to tell stories just by listening and telling stories over and over the way they had heard them told or by making them up on their own. It seemed that storytellers just naturally developed a sense of how and when to tell stories. Timing was paramount to their development as storytellers. It wasn't so much that you learned to tell a story a certain way, John Tofpi told me. You just had to be ready to tell one when the opportunity arose during conversation. That was the best way. For Kiowas, there was no special procedure for storytelling. The story event could take place anytime or anywhere in normal conversation. Storytellers learned to listen well and be ready to make a story in the midst of normal talk. In time you could become an expert. It was as natural a procedure as sneezing or clearing your throat, which, curiously enough, was often a signal that a story was about to be told.

Formulaic Openings and Closings

The earliest stories were clearly productions given in uncommon speech, for language takes on special coloring in storytelling that is different from common speech. Storytelling involves a special language code. The use of special codes "is one of the most widely noted characteristics of verbal art," writes Richard Bauman (1977), "so much so that special linguistic usage is taken often as a definitive criterion of poetic language.

Chapter IV ◎ Knowing How and When to Tell a Story

The special usage may center on one or another linguistic level or feature, or it may extend to whole codes" (p. 17). For storytellers like John Tofpi and Cornelius Spottedhorse, it would have been impossible to tell a story without somehow separating or encoding it a special way. When John or Cornelius told a story it came during ordinary conversation, but you could always tell the difference. There was a change in voice tone or rhythm. Facial expressions and even bodily gestures too indicated the presence of a narrative. All communication that took place within the story frame was understood as part of the performance (Bauman 1986). Listeners knew when a story began. They understood how it opened and closed. They knew the formulaic story framing in traditional Kiowa narratives. The frame was a performative device that was distinct from normal conversation and signaled that something important was being said.

When English speakers use the introductory formula "Once upon a time" they are making a distinction between everyday speech and a story. People produce performative language like this to separate what they are saying from normal conversation, to make listeners take notice. If people were to use everyday language when they told stories or recited, their words would fall on deaf ears. It is within that framework that stories were told in the Kiowa oral tradition that has come down to us today. As Bauman has pointed out, "Modern theories of the nature of verbal art tend overwhelmingly to be constructed in terms of special patterns within texts" (p. 7). That is, there is a concern with the form of expression rather than the needs of communication as the essence of verbal art (Bascom 1965).

"Séndé áhêl" (Séndé was coming along) is the formulaic opening in Séndé tales. Nobody knows who invented it or the formulaic closing, but they are still used when Kiowas tell Séndé stories. I have also found in almost all the stories I collected the ubiquitous hàu (yes). Hàu is the repetitive response listeners use to inform the storyteller they are following what he is saying. It appears to be more of a signal for the storyteller to continue than an affirmation. So crucial is this special code marker that it seems utterly impossible to tell a story without its inclusion.

The following story, Fàihêjègà (The Story of the Sun), illustrates, I believe, the best use of the formulaic opening and closing in traditional Kiowa storytelling. Note the opening, *Cáuigú á cí:dê* (The Kiowas were camping), and the closing hàu (yes; keep going).

The Kiowas were camping and there was no sun. There were strangers who possessed the sun and played with it all the time. They rolled it about and threw it high into the air. They gambled with it. When somebody came around they became very possessive of the sun and fussed over it.

One time somebody came and they did not leave and so the strangers let them play. There was a man, a deer, a prairie hawk, and a mythical coyote, and by and by they picked up the sun and ran away with it.

"Stand in line and pass it along," they cried.

The sun was hot and they had to toss it back and forth. Then Séndé stepped up and said, "Bring it here."

And they gave the sun to him and he kicked it straight up into the sky where it landed and all the world was lit up.

Yes you must say.

Chapter V

Telling Stories within Stories

"I need stories for the field study I'm doing, Sègî," I told Uncle Oscar one summer morning in 1998. He and I had arranged to meet at my mother and father's home in Carnegie to talk about Kiowa storytelling. Oscar Tsoodle was perhaps one of the last truly traditional Kiowa speakers alive. I addressed him in Kiowa (sègî means uncle or nephew) to set the mood and to put him at ease. At the time I had planned to record as many stories as I could in Kiowa. I'd already recorded John Tofpi and meant to go back and talk with him again. I wanted to be sure I had everything I needed in the way of the texts themselves, transcribed and translated, in order to examine how Kiowas told stories. So far I had seen that Kiowas were telling stories about everyday affairs. There were stories everywhere. They were being framed by different kinds of contexts all the time. You couldn't tell where one story left off and where another began. You had to listen closely or you could miss out on a great deal. I was progressively learning about Kiowa storytelling as it was happening. It wasn't what I expected. This is not to say Kiowas have quit telling the old stories, the ones told in Kiowa, the heroic stories of Séndé and his ilk. But these contemporary stories are about minor events in Kiowa life and are nothing like the heroic tales from my boyhood. Many I heard were personal narratives about relatives, brothers-in-law, and cousins doing funny things either to themselves or to other people. Joking and teasing dominated much contemporary storytelling. Sometimes it seemed that Kiowas weren't telling stories at all but telling jokes. It hadn't occurred to me how storytelling, the process of storytelling, was taking place until I sat down and took the time to observe and participate in it. I had to extend my own self by entering into the dialogue. I had to help the story develop at times by offering up my own comments and anecdotes.

Storytelling is a dynamic, existential creature. Hard to get a hold of. Difficult to recognize. When I first asked Uncle Oscar to tell me a story, he said he knew a few but then talked about other things. How was I to know that he'd already opened up a storytelling event? He changed the subject as if he wanted to think about it for a while first. But all along, while I waited, he told one story after another, and I had to be quick enough to catch on or miss out altogether.

Uncle Oscar studied me a moment.

"I want to know all I can about storytelling," I repeated.

"There's lots of prayers down here. You know that, don't you?"

I nodded my head. Hàu. I wanted to use as much Kiowa as I could for practice but also to keep as much of our dialogue Kiowa as possible.

"There are, Sègî. All up and down this creek. All of this land. Your grandpas and them—we had peyote meetings up and down this creek. There's lots of prayers on this land."

"Hàu."

Uncle Oscar gestured about with his hands as he talked. I thought, He's doing this in order to more clearly imagine the ground around us, where my grandfather had built his house and now where my mother's house stood. It was as if he needed to establish common ground before he could really talk about things. He wanted familiarity of terrain. He was using the home place as a reference point in order to come to terms with present time and his own recollection of events right here long ago. Kiowas know and love the geography around them. Sépyàldà (Rainy Mountain) is a point of reference for Kiowas for all times (Momaday 1969, Boyd 1981, 1983). It is the place where Kiowas ended up in their long migrations across the Plains. There are hundreds of other such geographical locations on the Plains from Montana to Mexico, but Sépyàldà is the granddaddy of them all, so to speak.

Chapter V ◎ Telling Stories within Stories

After he explained his reasons for wanting to come down to the old home place to talk, Oscar got into a serious frame of mind. He could do that in the twinkling of an eye. He changed gears so easily and had an engaging power over his listeners. He could lead us along like blind men into a land of mystery and delight. Kiowas and just about everybody else around Carnegie knew him. He was opinionated about almost everything. If you engaged him in conversation you might hear almost anything. You did not know what would come out of his mouth sometimes. He knew no strangers. That was one of his best qualities. If you were new in Carnegie and walked up to Uncle Oscar and asked him directions, he would tell you right away what you needed to know. He would also tell you all about the person you were looking for or the place you were going. That's what made him the attractive person he was. In Carnegie, which is mostly made up of whites, he talked with anybody anytime. He was complex, a human being with many sides to his personality, and he shared every part of himself with whomever he encountered.

After he established a common point of reference, Uncle Oscar began to talk about our relatives, how they were doing, where they were going, and so on. Kiowas, when they get together, invariably take up the subject of their own relatives. It is storytelling, a way of getting at the business of telling other stories. Since many of the stories Kiowas tell have to do with relatives, storytellers will begin talking right away about their own kin. At one point Oscar asked me a few direct questions about myself. He was warming up to me, I remember thinking. He wanted to get intimate real fast, I thought. That way he could say what he wanted to. We could be on common ground. He could relax, put me in my proper Kiowa place so I would have to listen to everything he had to say that day. It was a good way. It was the Kiowa way, I remember thinking.

My father was talking when Oscar interrupted him. Apparently, M., who is Oscar's granddaughter in the Kiowa way, had asked him the meaning of her name. "Well, what is it?" he had asked her in Kiowa. "Kòmjòmá [Ghost Woman]," she had said. "*Háun àn chólàu ém k*a*umâu* [People don't call themselves that kind of name]," he'd replied. You can talk about ghosts in stories or in dreams or some scary context but never as part of a real-life situation like a name.

"Kiowas don't call themselves ghosts," Oscar fairly growled in the way he does that reminds me of distant dark thunder.

"Hàu," said my father.

"Hàu," said my mother.

"Hàu," we all said together.

Peanut barked in the next room.

"That name is reserved for somebody dead," said my mother.

"Sure it is," Oscar agreed. "You can't use that name. Not Kiowas." His face darkened with a consternation I hadn't seen in a person's face in a long time. For a moment I thought he might curse, which he was prone to do in any given moment, but he didn't this time. We all laughed. We were warming up for some good stories. We were all in good spirits.

"Yeah," Uncle Oscar went on, "Call me Ghost Woman. And I said, I will not call you such a name. No. *Háunê.*"

I spoke up then and said younger Kiowas don't know Kiowa enough to realize what they're doing.

"That's right," Oscar replied. "They don't. Like this." He picked up a slice of bread to illustrate. "You have to explain this bread to someone in order for them to know what *ébáu* [bread] is. Some Kiowas call it *egáu*. Ébáu, égáu, it doesn't matter. The whole point is it's bread. That's what they have to know."

Our talk about M.'s name and her confusion about its meaning had taken us into a discussion about the Kiowa language and how it was being misused nowadays. We agreed that many Kiowas, particularly the young, knew some words like *kòmjó* (ghost) but didn't know how to use them correctly in conversation. That spoken Kiowa is in decline is a pretty commonly known fact among Kiowas and others. But when nonspeakers make mistakes, speakers laugh or correct them too harshly. This causes the nonspeakers to refrain. I wanted to bring up this subject, but my father spoke before I could.

"Kiowa is going out of spoken use," he said.

"It's hard to catch on to Kiowa," Uncle Oscar assured us. "You got to be speaking it day and night, day and night. Teaching it is hard too. Lot of them Kiowas do it their own way. You don't understand what they're saying. Like she said, Kòmjòmá. That's not right. Kiowas are scared to use that word in everyday talk. Yeah. I will not call you that, I told her. Let someone else call you that."

"Yeah," spoke up my father. He had been sitting there taking in everything the old master was saying. He wanted to keep the story going.

"The old ones knew how to give a [Kiowa] name," he continued. "They did it right. Oh, by the way, brother-in-law. L.'s daughter over here, B., has a daughter. They're having a peyote meeting. She wants me to give her a Kiowa name at that meeting. Now, how am I going to do that? Yes, I told her. I will. I asked her about her relatives to get some clue about a name, you know. It's not easy, this naming business. I thought it over. She could do something, you know. Why doesn't she bring in the water in the morning? They're so young, but they want a Kiowa name. That's interesting. They want to do it prayerfully. For the future. That's what it is. That's it. They thought it over. They never come into a meeting. But they've decided to make a meeting for a name. How do we name someone then? Peyote prayers and name use. Why not call her Á:kı̣dàu:chài:mà [Flower Prayer Woman]? This peyote is a flower, you know. We call it different names, but this one is appropriate, you know. It's good that way, see."

"Yeah. Do it prayerfully," Oscar offered. "Do it the right way. It's the way it has to be done."

He paused. He looked at me. It was the first time today that he made a long, direct eye contact with me. I was almost afraid what he might say to me.

"Your name is Pànthái:dê [White Cloud], *hạ̀u?*"

"Hàu," I answered relieved. "*Châu à kạ́u* [that is how I am called]."

"And *càunqí* Áutpạ̀u:à: *kạ́u* [Weeping-Pausing-Coming Forth]?"

He was wanting to confirm that Weeping-Pausing-Coming Forth was my cousin's son's Kiowa name. It is the name of my great-grandfather Tenadooah. It is a holy name, a name you can bear with great honor.

"Yes," I said. "That's Henry's son's name."

"Hàu. They gourd dance, don't they?"

He was making a remark about the name Áutpạ̀u:à:, a name given to a child who liked to gourd dance. I sensed that he wondered how that might be. I should have asked him if he had named my cousin's son himself. I don't know who gave my great-grandfather's name away. It is such a beautiful name. It suggests a very faithful and prayerful man. The name must be very old and must have come down many centuries like many Kiowa names, I remember thinking.

"You know your grandpa and their father, they made prayers," Uncle Oscar explained. "It's there, that. You know God controls your life. He's there. You're going to enjoy it all your life. You will die too. An old man. Like your grandpa and them. They [the Kiowas] made fun of the old man [Tenadooah] because he prays all the time. Áutpáu:à:. That's what that name means. He's weeping, praying. They made fun of him. He cries and stops and prays. Èmhá:dèà: [He-Who-Comes-Invoking-the-Great–Spirit]. Bèlfán [Sore Mouth], Big Bow, and him, the old man, my grandfather, the two of them went exploring together. Like Daniel Boone. 'We went around. They fed us. They treated us good. Those tribes we visited on our journeys. We just go. We just go for the heck of it. Those tribes welcomed us too. I prayed and him, he sang. That's what we did when we went out. They treated us good. We never killed nothing or nobody. We were just travelers seeing what there was to see in the land. They were good to us. We never killed nobody. They were good to us.'"

Because I sensed it was okay to, I broke out of the story frame, or thought that I had, by asking him what Áutpáu:à: and Bèlfán were looking for. Later, I decided that my questions and comments while he or any of my other storytelling consultants were speaking were common within the storytelling framework. That is, there was no objection to these interjections during our talk.

"Yeah. They were *dàumsáumzè:mà* [going around just looking at the land]. They liked water," he explained. "Kiowas like water and things. They went looking for water and told people where it was. That's what they were doing. They went out like that and then came back and told the people things, how it was way out there."

Dennis Tedlock (1983) writes that "once a narrative is well under way, the possible openings actually chosen for the *eeso* (yes or proceed) response are most likely to be those in which the performer departs from the story proper to offer an interpretive aside" (p. 290). I allowed, or rather we all allowed, Uncle Oscar to make this "interpretive aside," which opened up the story enough to allow other listeners to participate in the ongoing narrative. My mother, for instance, who had been busy in the kitchen with the food, spoke up—participated in the ongoing narrative, that is—as she moved between the table where we men were seated and the kitchen, back and forth.

"Hey, they had interesting stories to tell," she said, as she set out plates of hot food and a pitcher of ice tea. She'd been busy ever since I arrived. I wanted her to sit down and join us because she seemed to be a little standoffish. But as soon as she made this remark she sat down. Peanut was nowhere to be seen. I looked under the table.

"Where's your pooch?"

My mother looked up. "She's asleep. Leave her alone." As soon as she spoke, Peanut barked somewhere in a back room, and we all laughed.

"I bet they had interesting stories to tell," my mother said in Kiowa.

"Sure they did," Oscar remarked.

Yes, I thought. We are getting into some serious storytelling. You can feel the tension growing up around the table like a body of rising water. Any minute we're going to be up to our throats in it. Who needs Peanut at this important Kiowa moment? I braced myself for some good storytelling. I was excited about what I was going to hear, just as I used to be when I was a boy. When grandpa or any of the other old men told stories like this I remember how good it used to feel.

"They did," Oscar reiterated. "That's the way they were. Them two. They liked to see things, what was out there on the land. It's a big land, you know."

"I bet they learned a lot of things from different tribes," my mother added. Uncle Oscar was leaving his story open so his listeners could enter any time they wanted and contribute their own thoughts or comments. This is when Kiowa storytelling becomes the dynamic event that it is, I learned. When these added comments start coming, the level of the storytelling rises. Depending on the skillfulness of the storyteller, the story can remain open for a considerable time. The real test is how long the storyteller can hold out and sort of tease the listener along. A non-Indian listener would get restless or possibly annoyed at this point. I, in my impatience, have gotten angry with my grandfather who could hold off for a very long time. Sometimes he would stop a telling altogether so he could smoke a cigarette or change the subject. Then I would have to just sit back and wait until he was good and ready to start up again. When he left a story open, he could have been waiting for something in his narrative to catch up: an explanation, a definition, some other extraneous information. Or he might have needed me to make some comment or response, which I didn't always do. The point is that the story seemed to halt, and there you had to wait until it picked up again. At this juncture it is difficult to see exactly who the storyteller is, if you aren't alert. This day, the fact that Uncle Oscar was the invited guest and the object of my study reminded us. But an unexpected guest could have changed the situation, could have become the storyteller, at least for a time.

"Hàu," Oscar assured us. "They sure did. They went everywhere, them two. They were world travelers back then. They met different tribes, ø jógà [he said]."

After this last remark he stopped. He'd said what he wanted, I think. Perhaps he was pausing so somebody else could pick up from there. As soon as he stopped, my father spoke up.

"Now this business about Jé:gàcùngà [Pueblo dancing]," my father said, changing the subject. "That's what we call the snake dance? Hau?"

I looked at my father. In his mideighties, he was not only a good Kiowa speaker and tribal historian but also an excellent interlocutor. He knew how to keep things going in the right direction. He knew instinctively that we'd probably exhausted our talk about relatives and that we needed to move on to other things. I was glad he was there with us today.

"Hàu," Oscar replied, taking up dad's question. "Yes, Jé:gàgùn," he repeated. "Around here we call it snake dance now. That's wrong. It's not that. It's Jé:gàcùngà."

I asked how the Pueblos danced the snake dance.

Chapter V ◎ Telling Stories within Stories

"Hàu," he said. "They dress up. Men and women. It's a Pueblo dance, you know. They dance it with dignity. Not like we do now. Snake dance. We changed it from its original form."

What he in fact meant was we ruined it. Originally it was a dignified dance with meaning, but when the Kiowas took it they made it into something different. That is what was irritating to him.

"We ruined it, didn't we?" I said, hoping he would open up a new story perhaps. Technically, the story frame had broken slightly to include yet another story. For the time being I wasn't sure what might be going on. I had but to wait and see what would follow next.

"Hàu. We sure did," everybody around the table agreed in one voice after a moment. "It's not the way it used to be."

"How did they do the Jé:gàcùngà?" I asked, encouraged by the group.

"Well, not like they do it now. Different. They sang the same songs." Oscar proceeded to sing a snake dance song. It was short. Peanut joined us under the table by barking while he sang.

"Darn dog." My mother got up and took her pet to her bedroom. She shut the bedroom door and joined us at the table again.

When Oscar stopped singing he explained, "They held feathers in their hands like this. They dressed up good too. They danced well. With feathers. All adults. Get them damn kids out of there! They don't know. It's a serious dance. It is."

"Hàu," we all agreed.

Peanut reappeared under the table. She smiled up at us. Then she wagged her tail. As she did, her whole body wagged with her tail. When she finished she yawned and lay down in a heap beside my mother's feet. I watched my mother's tiny dog, amused at how much my mother loved small dogs. Her previous love, Chi-chi, a chihuahua too, hated men. And snapped at passing feet from underneath the dining room table. Peanut, on the other hand, wanted every visitor to be her best friend. She had an even temper and tolerated both men and women and even strangers who came to my mother's house. As I thought about my mother's dog I thought about all of the Kiowa dog stories I had heard. Grandpa said dogs talked a long time ago. "They just knew how," he explained. "They understand Kiowa. Don't say anything bad about a dog. He'll remember and take it out on you some day when you least expect it."

Most Kiowas love dogs. I remember seeing lots of dogs at Kiowa homes. When you drove up to somebody's house, they'd come out by the dozens. All kinds of them. Lean ones, fat ones, old ones, young ones, puppies, bony, starving, mean, noisy, dumb, smart. There were as many kinds of Indian dogs as there were people. No wonder there were so many Kiowa dog stories. Dogs are four-legged Kiowas.

There followed a long interlude. We were drinking coffee but hadn't started to eat yet. We were looking at the food my mother had set out for us when Uncle Oscar spoke up again.

"Over here at Óhòmàu,[1] Father came along. He was all dressed up and I said, You ought to give me that outfit and let me dance. You're a white man, I said."

"Why did he come?" I laughed.

"Yeah," Uncle Oscar went on. "He ruined it. I made fun of him. He's got his own place. I notice Catholic priests try to do our things.[2] Several times I've seen it. They want to know the way we do things. At the fair, you know that priest said he's making a peyote meeting and invited me. He said, This peyote. How does one get peyote? That Navajo I was with was going to tell him and I told him not to. No, brother, I said. There's no way, I said. He doesn't know. This one doesn't know. He doesn't need to know. This Navajo wants to know how we do it too. After one meeting he was running he said, Hey, brother, I'm going to go over to this powwow. He wanted to run off just like that. We just got out of the meeting. You don't mix things up like that, you know. They mix everything up. They don't do it right. That's not the way. You know, they ruin stuff. Even the food isn't the right kind. Chili. They had chili and I said, We don't eat chili like that."

"They don't know," my father added. "They do it all wrong. They eat early and then go home," he complained. "I don't understand them." He didn't like the hurry people seemed to be in when they ran a peyote meeting, he said. Both he and Oscar complained about how the peyote ritual was changing, that nobody did things right, the way they should. People weren't only ignorant about the correct procedures, they were also in too big of a hurry. As soon as the meeting was over, Oscar said, that Navajo man got up and went to Sunday church services the next morning. "You don't do things like that," he said.

The sun was high in the east sky. It was a clear, hot day. The locusts were beginning to warm up their midsummer songs in the creek trees a little way from my mother's house.

"I asked the Navajo man where his father's symbolic peyote was and he said he didn't know," Oscar explained.[3]

"They don't know," my father added. "Háunê."

"They said, Eat now. It's chili. I don't eat chili, I told them."

Uncle Oscar, although he didn't say so, was referring presumably to a meeting he'd attended that the Navajo man had conducted and to which he had invited a Catholic priest. I had to listen closely to figure out who he was talking about and where all the action was taking place. It was hard to follow but exciting nevertheless.

"You too," explained Oscar. "Smoke. If it's a woman, you let her smoke it. It's a woman's smoke. You can roll your own after she's finished. It's her *tà:bàut* [tobacco]. You keep it on your own side."

"If you bring in *tó:* [water], it's the same way," my father interjected. "There's a certain order to things. If you go outside, don't go outside and smoke."

"Hàu. Smoke in there," said Oscar. "Take your time. Take your time."

Here he emphasized time once more. Like most modern Americans, Kiowas nowadays are in a hurry, he complained. In earlier times, everyday life went along at a slower pace, he said. There was more time to talk, more time to listen, more time to sing, dance, eat, and visit. I should add here that one of the biggest complaints I heard among the people I recorded and interviewed was that the modern Kiowas, like white people, "lived in the fast lane." This remarkable shift in lifestyle was not confined to only young Kiowa people: every living Kiowa was caught up in things that weren't Kiowa. Many of my consultants were surprised that people their age and older had stopped taking time to talk and visit with one another.

And so Oscar and my father complained that the celebrants disrupted the peyote service by going outside to smoke. If somebody wanted to smoke, he or she could take time and do it right by smoking inside the tipi. The right way. Things were changing, and these two oldtimers didn't like it. They didn't like that Catholic priest who went into a meeting anytime he wanted to. Or the fact that one of the celebrants would just get up after a meeting and go to church the next morning, as if the peyote meeting itself had little or no spiritual value at all. If you prayed all night, then what was the point of going out the next day to pray at church?

Things were coming apart in Kiowa life, and Uncle Oscar and my father weren't so angry as they were disappointed. Oscar would make a comment and then my father would follow by making one himself. Oscar opened up the conversation for my father to enter it, back and forth and so on. Each time one opened up the conversation, the other threw in a comment or anecdote or story.[4] It was a well-orchestrated demonstration of how these two Kiowas could let a story occur almost casually any time in conversation. This going back and forth struck me as uniquely Kiowa. At a follow-up meeting between the two of them during the Fourth of July powwow at Carnegie, they did the same thing. My father began a conversation about how Kiowas were now participating poorly in the gourd dance. Uncle Oscar got his cue somewhere during this time and told a story right in the midst of my father's talk. Their one-on-one conversation soon brought in Oscar's nephew and several other Kiowas who happen to be sitting nearby in the shade arbor. Everybody there got a chance to contribute. The conversation opened up enough for any bystander to add an anecdote or two. It was a total dialogic event. Kiowas love dialogic settings that engender stories.

Another important point I'd like to make here is about smoking in public places. In 1998, many public places posted signs to warn smokers where they cannot smoke. A thoughtful Kiowa smoker, rather than light up in a tipi, would likely go outside away from nonsmokers, thus not violating laws. This idea didn't occur to me until my wife, Carolyn, suggested it. In the old days, celebrants almost always stayed inside the tipi to smoke. The public smoking issue might have been one reason

Chapter V ◎ Telling Stories within Stories

people now went outside to smoke. If I had suggested that, however, Oscar would no doubt have made a number of critical comments that I believe would still burn my ears: Oh, you know how them young Kiowas are, he might have said. Or, They have no respect. Them old Kiowas. They smoke anytime they want to. They don't care about the old ways. Like it used to be. They're selfish. They just think about themselves. They're just a bunch of renegades. They do anything they want these days. It ain't like it used to be.

"When they pray, say hàu," dad said, as the discussion continued about the Kiowa peyote way. "Hàu. That's the idea. You agree in there. That prayer will be done. You're in there for that."

"*Chólhàu* [That's right]," added Oscar shaking his head. He was on a roll now. If there were going to be any good stories told, now was the time, I thought.

"That's what it's all about in that tipi," he said. He was going to say something else, but we were ready to eat now, my mother announced. So she prayed and we began to eat. Oscar and my father went on talking about the Kiowa peyote way, and I sat there and helped myself to my mother's boiled beef tongue and potatoes. I ate and tried to listen to everything I could. After they finished talking about the peyote way, I asked Oscar if it would be okay to record some of his stories now. I had asked him several times before, and he had agreed but wouldn't tell any stories at that point. I think he wanted to think things over before he got started, which is pretty typically Kiowa. Still, on the other hand, the storytelling had already ensued. We were in the midst of it. Once we sat down at the table that morning, storytelling officially commenced. When doing fieldwork with the Western Apaches, Keith Basso (1990) found that he had to wait several days or even weeks before he got one "identifi-able" story recorded. I, too, wanted what in my mind was an identifiable story. I was in the same predicament as Basso. From the minute Oscar walked into my mother's house, we'd entered storytelling. Everything that we said and everything we did around the table was storytelling and part of a bigger story picture. Everything was contextualized into story. But there was no single identifiable story to record. Uncle Oscar had come prepared in his own way for this storytelling session and slowly swept us all into the narrative framework he had built up. But it took many months for me to realize what had happened that hot summer afternoon.

"I want to record something," I said again. I set down my coffee cup. I adjusted the tape recorder to make sure it was working. "If it's all right with you, Sègî. You know, the old stories you heard when you were a boy."

Oscar paused, a cup of coffee in his hand. A point of light shone in his eyes like a distant sun. "Like my kǫ́ [grandpa] used to tell me?" My favorite Kiowa uncle laughed.

I told him hàu. I was glad he'd finally decided to tell a "real" story.

"Yes. That's what I want to hear, Sègî." I pressed on. I don't know if I said it at the time, but if I could go back right now to mom's house and we were all sitting around again, I think I would tell him I wanted to find out how old Kiowas told stories a long time ago and that I wanted him to show me how it was done.

Oscar sipped his coffee and smiled. Like any good Kiowa he was taking his time. I had a lot of respect for this man, I remember thinking. He was good, my favorite Tenadooah. I remembered him from when I was a boy. He used to come around and visit Grandpa at the old house that sat on the bank of the creek. He came at any season, but I see him better in the soft light of summer, perhaps in the evening when the western sky is rosy colored and the air is filled with the scent of wildflowers that were always growing luxuriantly along the creek north of the house. They talked about old times. He knew many things about our huge and growing Tenadooah family and was himself becoming an important Kiowa. Lots of people knew him. Both Indian and non-Indian. These days, he is considered a traditional Kiowa because he is a peyote man. He is one of the last fluent Kiowa speakers. Some years ago, when he found out I was working closely with Parker McKenzie and the Kiowa language he laughed. "He doesn't know anything. He's a Mexican.[5] What does he know?" I had laughed and tried to understand what he was saying. I wanted to defend my old friend Parker. Still, in the end, I knew Oscar cared a great deal about the language and had a lot of respect for Parker. He was just playing the role of a Kiowa relative to me. He was letting me know how important it was that we understood the other Kiowas around us, had our own ideas about ourselves and our own language, and didn't need someone outside our immediate family telling us what to do. I felt honored sitting there in my mother's house listening to him. I knew I was in for some very special surprises.

Uncle Oscar asked me to get him an ashtray and lit up a Marlboro cigarette. As he lit up and began to puff I thought about that Marlboro cowboy riding out on the open range. In my mind's eye I saw Oscar jump on the back of the Marlboro cowboy's saddle and ride away with him. When I looked up again his eyes were shut tightly. He seemed to be asleep, but he still had that cigarette clutched between his teeth. There was a grin on his face. By now, several hours had elapsed, and I could see he had been working up the inspiration to tell a story in the good old Kiowa way.

"Not to change the subject," he began suddenly in Kiowa, "but how old are your children? Ah, how, how big are they? *É syânè: è tháu:* [When they were small you all lived here]."

I told him their ages, and he laughed jovially. He looked like a great Greek god sitting there in the big armchair. His face dark as a walnut and round. It looked as if he had greased it well with some kind of oil. He said he couldn't believe they were as old as I said. Even my father and mother were surprised. They grow up too fast, they both remarked.

"Yes. Before you know it," I said.

Kiowas are so very proud of their relatives, especially the young. They can go on for hours talking about children in the family. Children are a great source of pride for Kiowas. Children are the future, and Kiowa parents and grandparents try every way they can to see that their children receive the best preparation for a good and productive life. People from the outside cannot see this family pride, I know. But it is there every time I sit down with Kiowas and we talk about their families and children. Kiowas are like parents and grandparents everywhere. It just seems that for Kiowas there is nothing better than to have a child or grandchild who is healthy and growing up and doing something significant and important in the world. They have special pride in children who have gone somewhere away from the community and are doing well.

Uncle Oscar listened carefully as I tried as best I could to tell him in Kiowa about my children. His round face brightened in pleasure to hear how well my children were doing. I knew he and my parents approved of my conversing in Kiowa. They like it when younger Kiowas speak the language. Sometimes they chuckle when words are mispronounced or misapplied in speech.[6] Many younger Kiowas fear ridicule when they speak, but in most instances, Kiowa elders think well of their attempts. As one man told me the other day at the Kiowa Elders Center: "You have to try. It doesn't hurt. Make all the mistakes you want. We all make mistakes." I liked that. It reassured me. And even though I am perhaps one of the youngest fluent Kiowa speakers around, my Kiowa is not perfect. I can expect to be corrected by kinsmen when I speak. I had to overcome my fear of making mistakes a long time ago, and that has helped me speak more now.

"You know, Sègî," said Uncle Oscar, "before you know it you and your wife will be living by yourselves." He looked at me as if he wanted me to respond, but I only nodded my head. He then began to talk about his own wife and their life together. The story frame he was constructing grew larger.

"Yes, we were close," he assured us in Kiowa. "She bore us children. You and your wife will be by yourselves before you know it." His voice took on a graver tone. "You'll be living by yourselves."

When he shifted to the subject of my wife and me, I was suddenly drawn back into his story. "It'll be quiet after your children grow up and leave," he cautioned me. "You'll be alone."

Yes, I thought, and nodded my head.

As he continued I couldn't help thinking how our conversation shifted back and forth from story to present life and back to story. I immediately thought about something Dennis Tedlock (1983) said about Zuni storytelling: "The more a fieldworker knows and is known, the less that fieldworker can avoid joining the action. The other side of this is that the less that a fieldworker knows and is known, the greater will be that fieldworker's inability to interpret the actions of others, whether those actions take him into account or not" (p. 287). Kiowas tell stories in the same

Chapter V ◎ Telling Stories within Stories

manner as Zunis. Participation is required. No wonder Oscar kept bringing me into his stories. He was expecting me to contribute to the story
in some way. This kind of shifting from story back to present time continued for the rest of the afternoon, when he finally did tell me the story
about the mother deer and her song.

Chapter VI

Teasing, Joking, Telling the Biggest Fib

Hey, lookit that chief eat that sonavabitch, will you!

"I've got a real good one to tell you," Cornelius Spottedhorse laughs.

He, John Tofpi, Wilbur Kodaseet, and I are sitting in overstuffed chairs in a corner in the Kiowa Elders Center one summer morning. There are potted plants in coffee cans beside the huge hearth. We are surrounded by photos of old Kiowas. The photos came from the Oklahoma Historical Society and the Western History Collection at the University of Oklahoma. The four of us arrived a few minutes ago and are enjoying coffee and talking about just anything that comes to mind. Someone observes that the figure in one of the photos is a relative. A few elderly Kiowas, ready for the noon meal, are sitting here and there in deep armchairs talking quietly among themselves.

"I know several good ones," John T. says.

"I know one too," somebody says across the way. Someone is always wanting to tell a story. When word got out that I was recording Kiowa stories, Kiowas came crawling out from under every proverbial rock. I was flattered that so many wanted to be a part of the study but ended up selecting just a few.

"You go," John T. tells Cornelius.

"You ready?" Cornelius looks at me.

Chapter VI ◎ Teasing, Joking, Telling the Biggest Fib

I turn on the tape recorder and set the volume. "All right." Cornelius, who uses a pair of crutches to get around, is a very able storyteller, whom I heard when I worked at the Center some years back. A big man, Cornelius is a very comical person and someone I have always enjoyed. When I first met him in the 1980s, he struck me as extremely intelligent and about as well informed about Kiowa life and the goings-on around Kiowa country as John Tofpi.

You know this man went up to that church. R.'s church. You know him, don't you? Well, he's back. He went way up there to preach and then came back home. That R.'s married to that T. You know her. Anyway, this one [John Tofpi] went up to that church to hear him preach and R. told him all about it. Well, this one got so wrapped up in that preaching he went home that night and he traveled to heaven. Well, he was up there and the first person he met was his grandpa. His hair was all long and sticking up. He didn't brush it. And he was all dirty and stringy. The first thing he said when he saw this one was, "Hey, do they still eat raw *bót* [cow innards] down there?"

This story is a hyperbolic, comic tale. Cornelius doesn't tell us John T. dreamed and went to heaven. He just says he traveled to heaven. I had to think a few seconds before I realized what he was talking about. As far as Cornelius was concerned, John really went up there and saw his grandfather. The joke of the whole matter is of course the question about Kiowas still eating bót. Presumably, when John's grandfather was alive, the Kiowas relished the delicacy. Now that he is dead he is supposedly longing for bót and wondered if the Kiowas still prize it as of old. To get the full import of this comical tale, one has to understand the cultural implications of this very special food.[1] Many Kiowas, when they butcher cattle, take the tender innards, including the kidneys and liver, and devour them right there on site. I have heard Cornelius tell this story about four different times over a six-month period. He tells it almost the same way each time. The story contains the same characters. All the action is the same, and there is the same punch line. He made up the story, of course, but I always get so caught up in it that it seems that it must actually have occurred.

Telling Stories ◎ the Kiowa Way

The next story is a real Kiowa comic classic because it has been told by many Kiowas for many years. It is about a real event that took place around Gotebo, Oklahoma, around the turn of the century perhaps, when many Kiowas lived on their allotments near and around small rural towns like Gotebo. Cornelius tells the story almost exclusively in English. But he adds just enough Kiowa words for the comical subtleties. In telling this second story, he becomes more animated and adds his own personal twists and humorous comments. When it comes to telling humorous stories, Cornelius Spottedhorse is stylistically hard to beat.

Three Kiowas were out hunting and they killed a buffalo. Boy, they proceeded to butcher it and one of them was eating this piece of the innards. I don't know what they call it but it's a piece about this size [gestures with his hands]. It looks like a gland or something and while he's cutting it up and putting it in his mouth, two Wild West cowboys ride up. "Hey, chief, what you got there?" one of them cowboys says. But he's too busy eating that thing he doesn't even look up. Golly, that White man just shakes his head like he can't believe that Indian, watching him gorge down that thing, and his buddy looks over at him and says, "Hey, lookit that chief eat that sonavabitch, will you!"
Ever since then, Kiowas call that bót sonavabitch.[2]

Telling Taller Tales

When Cornelius finishes telling this story, he belly laughs. John Tofpi laughs. We all laugh. By now, several other Kiowas have joined us. They hear Corn's story and laugh. It is an excellent Kiowa joke story. The joke is on all of us Kiowas of course. We are all the butt end of this funny tale because we Kiowas still call that piece of cow entrail sonavabitch. This term is not offensive. It is humorous because a white man coined the name. The Kiowas heard the word and took it as their own. Kiowas look for such ironic twists in everyday life. They make good material for stories. Some of the stories I collected are accounts like this one. They do not all involve white people, but when they do they are especially funny, I think, because Kiowas like to juxtapose white and Indian words, ideas, and thought. Many of these comical accounts recall tall tales like those

Chapter VI ◎ Teasing, Joking, Telling the Biggest Fib

Richard Bauman (1986) collected in Texas. All involve comical occurrences between two or more people. They are often outright lies. That is their special appeal. Bauman calls such stories "orally performed verbal art," and he focuses on how these performances draw significantly from their social contexts. He writes that his investigations grew out of his "long-standing interest in the ethnography of oral performance . . . as a way of speaking, a mode of verbal communication" (p. 2). Like some of the best storytelling analyses, his work follows in the tradition of such figures as Edward Sapir, Kenneth Burke, Mikhail Bakhtin, and Roman Jakobson, "who have maintained an integrated vision of the social and the poetic in the study of oral literature" (p. 2). What makes the Texas stories humorous are the inside jokes that the storyteller and the listener know. Storyteller and listener share a social context as they do in Kiowa narrative performances.

After Cornelius finishes his little tale, in order not to be outdone, John Tofpi himself proceeds to tell his own version of the same story. It is as if he wants to tell it the *right way* this time. I know the practice. I have sat in on some storytelling sessions in which two or more people tell the same story but a slightly different way each time. Each tries to tell the most fantastic version. On almost every occasion, I sensed a bit of competition. I think trying to outdo one another is part of the fun, just as the teasing is.

John T. finishes, and in a few minutes Cornelius tells yet another version of the same story. They are building the story in ways to make it even more hilarious than it was the time before. They are trying to see who can tell the most humorous version in the most exaggerated way. Cornelius changes the characters slightly and puts John T. in the middle of the bót story. He recontextualizes for added comic effect. William A. Foley (1997) would say he was recontextualizing from some past source to create a new interaction in the story. My grandfather would sometimes put me into a Séndé story and make me feel as if I was part of the drama. He would have me say something to which Séndé or one of the animals would respond. To bring the listener into close contact with the story elements, if not to let him play a bit part, is all part of the entertainment and fun. It is an effective storytelling method not confined to Kiowas. It works in both oral and written narratives. The funny thing in Cornelius's retelling was that John was now among the Kiowas butchering the cow when the cowboys came along, his hungry eyes glowing.

As expected, we all laugh and joke about cow innards after Cornelius finishes his short story. By now the big room is humming with voices of elderly Kiowas the way it does each day as the Center fills. The sound is like the rush of distant water out of the hills. Indeed, it is a pleasant sound because the voices are those of people you know well or who are kin to you in that special Kiowa way. We are creating quite a disturbance in our storytelling corner and attracting a few of the curious. I look around. We have caught the attention of an old man. He shambles toward us smiling, his hand extended. After I shake his hand, he nods his ancient silvery head and totters back to a chair and sits down. Some of the other new arrivals come over to shake our hands and pay their respects. Goodwill fills the big room like a warm substance. Everywhere there is a feeling of an unnameable joy. I am glad I came today. This, I tell myself, is a truly Kiowa environment and I am right smack in the middle of it. It seems we have struck the right chord today. We have created a perfect Kiowa environment right here. Would that some great ethnographer like Mooney or Malinowski would walk up suddenly to experience all of this and then write about it! I ask myself: Is this really happening? Does it always happen? To Kiowas? To others? Is this how Kiowas come together and tell stories? Is this what those cultural anthropologists experience out in the field when they immerse themselves in observation-participation? Is it that simple? Yes. It is a historic time, and we are all alive in it. This is the fulfillment of something inexpressible. It is holistic and sacred. Àhó! It is the Kiowa way. Hàu, I feel blessed today.

Telling Stories One on One

Another time Cornelius and I, just the two of us, meet in the same spot at the Center. This time we're alone. John Tofpi is in Lawton. He collected his allotment lease money and went to pay his bills. Cornelius is in a more somber mood this time and relates mostly in English the following story about an incident south of where we are:

I want to tell you about this man. This man. Yale Spottedbird was telling the story about the Kiowas going way down there. Texas. They stopped at that big river. I think they call it the Brazos. Brazos River. Váuêl, they said. They know where to cross. They happened to look across and there was an Indian man, strange Indian man. Sitting across. Way over there. And of course, they're Kiowas. *Hégáuigáu* [inexplicably] they want to get rid of him. So one went around this way. One went way this way. And they got across and knocked him on the *áultêm* [head]. They hit him!

So they rested there. They went on south. Way down in south Texas. Coming back, at that river crossing, he was still there. He was still alive! So they got him for good this time. So when they came back [to their home camp] this guy named his son Áàui:hòlhèl [They-Who-Killed-Him-Again].

See? That's the *hê:jègà* [story].

"They came back and that guy was alive and they really killed him then. I don't know how it happened. It's kind of like magic, ain't it? It's funny, ain't it? They thought they got him the first round, see. But he came alive. So, they named his son Áàui:hòlhèl, They-Who-Killed-Him-Again.[3]

"That's a good story," I say.

"Yes, it is."

"I wonder why they killed that man?" I don't want to believe these Kiowas are so bloodthirsty, so I ask Cornelius how anybody could just snuff out somebody's life.

"Well," Cornelius replies, "the stories come out like that, you know. He was just sitting there. Doing nothing. When they came back he was still sitting there after they hit him over the head. The Kiowa warriors couldn't believe he was still alive, I guess, and must have been astonished. They had hit him over the head with an axe like that and thought he was dead as a doorknob, but when they come back they find him sitting up just like he was the first time. Gyah! It's bad, ain't it?"

"I'll say."

"Hey, they were bad, ain't it?"

"I know it. They just killed him like that."

"They did. Ain't it funny how people are?"

"Yeah. It's bad."

"When they came back, I mean when them warriors come home he [apparently the Kiowa warrior who killed the stranger] named his own son after that man sitting there. Áàui:hòlhèl. That's what they called him. That's his name. They came back there and he was sitting there, that man, and they killed him again. Golly. It's bad, ain't it?"

"I'll say it is. They were commemorating what happened."

"Right," Cornelius agrees. "Those Kiowas. Bad, ain't it?"

"It is."

I sit there and have to think about what Cornelius has just told me about the Kiowas killing that hapless stranger. I reflect on it. I have to think about Áàui:hòlhèl, whose father had taken the murder and recontextualized it into his own life. What Cornelius seemed to be musing on was the strangeness of a man coming back to life; but even more, the irony of the murderer giving his own son a name commemorating the event. That must have been a very Kiowa thing to do. Cornelius mentions other instances of a name being conjured up. I mention the name Yí:sàum, Parker McKenzie's name, which recalls a heroic event, and tell how that name came to be. Kiowa names like Jòháu:sàn (Little Bluff), Zépgàuétjé (Big Bow), and others also represent some Kiowa experience. What has happened is the event has been abbreviated into its simplest, most intelligible parts, usually the root terms and the gender marker on the end, to create a name. When Kiowas get together and talk about a relative, say, they can often summon up the entire name.

"Them stories come out like that," Cornelius says. "Now, let me tell you this other story about this Kiowa butchering that took place sometime after the territory opened up to white people."

Them cowboys come riding up.

"What you doing?"

"We're going to eat."

From what I hear it's called—it's round. And some people they stuff it. And then some of them just cook it like that.

Chapter VI ◎ Teasing, Joking, Telling the Biggest Fib

And them *Tháukáui* [white people] said, "You eat that?"
"Yeah."
"Well, I'll be a sonavabitch," *jó:gà* [a cowboy said].
"Hyah! *Gàu há:chò ę́:gàu gá kàu:màu!* [Look. He's calling this thing sonavabitch!]

"That's how it got started," Cornelius laughs, referring to how sonavabitch came to be associated with cow innards. There must be thousands of such adopted terms, but no one has taken time to collect all of them and find out their derivations.

Cornelius has told this story before, and I recorded him several times. All the versions were more or less the same. This time I noticed he left out some of the details but not enough to change it drastically. In this version, he also provided more dialogue than he had previously. Many stories Kiowas tell can be told a different way, but the essential idea will remain intact. If it is a joke story, the punch line will of course be the same, but the story is often funnier at each retelling. The storyteller always tries to bring something extra into it so that it will be better than before. I enjoy the different versions of the same story told in a single session, as do other listeners. The story provokes laughter each time.[4]

On yet another occasion, another prelunchtime gathering in the Center that includes John T., Wilbur, and numerous elders awaiting their meal, I ask Cornelius to retell the John Tofpi story about going to heaven and visiting with his grandfather, just to see how much of the story content he will change this time, and I am not disappointed:

He [John T.] had a prayer meeting at his house. First time he ever had a prayer meeting at his house. He don't pray, you know. I told him after everybody left that he still wanted to be a real Indian. He went to heaven.

I want to see my grandpa, [he said].

After midnight.

I said, When you went up there did they have them Russian ships? Sputnik, you know.

He just laugh. He laughed about it. At his house this summer [R. the preacher] is going to come back. At his house. [The preacher's] wife T., her Indian name's T., she's got a little organ. It's got another name but it looks like a little piano. It lays right on her paunch. Boy howdy! She's a good singer, you know. She's a good singer. That one [T.], she's bringing it [the instrument].

I said [to John T.], You better get ready. [Have] lots of sandwiches, bananas, and Kool-Aid. Boy! And cake. Boy! Now [R. and his wife, T.] they're coming this summer, I told him. Be ready ahead of time.

This story does not even sound like the one he told us before. This time Cornelius doesn't say anything about the church where John T. supposedly went to hear R. preach. This time there is a prayer meeting at John T.'s own house. There are other people in this version. Cornelius suggests a surrealist scene with the Russian space satellite. And he gives us parts of the story rather than the whole thing and adds new details and characters as he goes along. I have noticed other Kiowa storytellers do that. Sometimes they seem to be trying to outdo a previous performance: they repeat words or phrases for emphasis, leave things out and add material so that you don't recognize what you did before. Cornelius does exactly this when he repeats "at his house" and "she's a good singer" and when he brings in T. and her little organ. He does it both in English and in Kiowa. The effect is the same.

Another variation in this second telling of the story is the direct contact with John T., who laughs almost all the way through the telling. Cornelius provokes him into making asides to the rest of us—He's lying. He's bad, ain't it? You believe him?—which add to the fun.

"Corn, that's a pretty good story," I say.

"It is, isn't it?" agrees Wilbur. He looks at John, who is still chuckling, and notices an old man who has just shambled up. The old man has a cup of coffee in his hand.

"I know some stories, son," the old man tells me.

"You do?" I remember that I've seen him before. He has a mop of silver hair. He's so stoop-shouldered it's a wonder he can move around as swiftly as he does.

I watch him return to a table where other elders have congregated. He tells them something in Kiowa, and they all laugh. I think about the old man in Cornelius's story, the first one. John T.'s grandfather. I wonder what he looked like. I wonder if John was as close to him as he seemed to be in the story. Did Cornelius know him? Were they related closely? I believe that John must have been very close to him. Typically Kiowa. Kiowa grandparents. Many of the stories I'd heard had grandparents in them. Everybody seemed to want you to know he had a grandpa or grandma who was like nobody else's.

"What do you think, brother?" John asks me. Over the months we've worked together, we have become exceedingly close partners. When Kiowas see us together they smile and greet us in special ways. I can't explain how. It just seems that people enjoy our relationship. Maybe they're amused that we are brothers. That he is much older than I.

"I think you'd better try to top this guy," I say. "How do you suppose you can do that?"

"Who me?" John gathers himself to his feet. He chuckles to himself as he goes to fetch himself some more coffee. I can hear him making a remark about himself to somebody. At the Kiowa Elders Center you never feel alone. Around noon the place is almost always packed with old people. They come in the front door, and right away they're shaking hands all around. The way some of them carry on, you'd think they haven't seen each other in a long time. It's a lot of fun watching them come and go. I must be an old hand at it. I've been around old people most of my life.

When John returns, Cornelius is already telling us another story. He doesn't even bother to look up when at least another half dozen elders gather around us in the corner.

As he picks up the story pace, I'm reminded of Uncle Oscar's storytelling style. He would begin slowly. Then, what seemed halfway through his narrative, or what you would make of it to be a narrative, he would speed up. It was a very effective way to keep your attention.

"How about that bridge?" Cornelius says, just as we are about to wrap up our session. I don't understand what he is talking about, and so I ask him.

"They're stupid, aren't they? Real goofy. They just stood there ogling. When they were dedicating that bridge down there, them Kiowas."

He is referring to the naming of a bridge west of Carnegie. The county roads commission had recently repaired the bridge, and a certain Kiowa preservation board had decided that the occasion warranted rededication and naming. The name the board members chose was Sétáfètjàu (Afraid-of-Bears), in honor of one of the leaders of the ghost dance of the 1880s, but the naming stirred controversy among tribal members because many of them deemed Sétáfètjàu unworthy. When I ask Cornelius what can be done about it, he tells me he doesn't know.

"They just named it," he says. "It don't make sense, does it?"

We talk about Sétáfètjàu, and I realize that I haven't heard of him myself. I think about the ghost dance. It came to the Kiowas in the late 1800s. Like tribes all over the country, the Kiowas were afraid that the whites were going to take over all the land. The Indians were losing everything so fast that they decided to do something about it. Some say there was a Paiute man named Wevoka, a holy man out west. He had a dream or vision. He supposedly started the ghost dance. Tribes around Paiute country picked it up. Almost overnight the ritual spread. Every tribe on the Plains wanted to dance the buffalo herds back to the ancient hunting grounds. Almost every Indian wanted to chase the whites back to where they came from. This was Indian country and nobody else had any business being here. This spiritual restlessness was akin to many apocalyptic movements you read about in the Bible and more obscure texts. When I think about the ghost dance and how the practitioners danced feverishly until they became overwrought and began to hallucinate and faint, I am reminded of the religious zealots in our own time and their quest for spiritual perfection or whatever they seek.

The actual sacred grounds where the Kiowas used to ghost dance are about three miles north of that bridge. I try to remember some of the names associated with the ritual but cannot. All I remember is how the ghost dance came from the north and how the Kiowas adopted it, hoping that it would restore them back to the lifestyle of the olden days. Many Kiowas believed that the buffalo would return like a great whirlwind. People who died would rise up from the earth everywhere and the white man would be chased away. The great herds of buffalo who were living inside the belly of Mount Scott would stampede out of the door on the north side in a steady stream until all the land was filled with them, just as the old stories promised.

While we are talking about the controversy surrounding the naming of that bridge, I think of the possibility of a story growing out of that event. Knowing Cornelius, I am sure he will have lots to say about that bridge naming. He'll fabricate. He'll put some of his friends into the action. Put dialogue into their mouths. Make them think about their relatives, their wives, their girlfriends.

"Yeah, they named that bridge just like that," Cornelius says. "I don't know about them Kiowas." He looks right at me. He has the most remarkable expression. His face is that of a man who has been looking for something very valuable and has just found it. Wilbur and John have gotten up and left us sitting there by ourselves. Most of the elders have gone in to eat. We're alone. Earlier I heard the sound of singing in the distant hills south of Carnegie. There is a big powwow going on out there. Maybe it's the ghost dancers of old. Could it be a sun dance? Is this the right season? Is there an encampment of Kiowas, a thousand tipis strong, along the course of that muddy Washita River?

"You ready to go home?"

I look at Cornelius, who seems satisfied with our session. I want to return so we can talk some more about storytelling. I want to find out what he thinks about the old origin narratives. Does he know any in Kiowa? Most Kiowas don't. I feel they don't. Every Kiowa elder I've asked to tell me some of those old stories has refused to. Or maybe they just want to share them with their own family. I should ask John T. But I don't think he knows them either. It's so sad that we Kiowas are losing some of the oldest stories about how Kiowas emerged from a nether world into one that was full of light and many beautiful things.

Chapter VII

Contextualizing and Recontextualizing Old Texts into New Texts

---

God created people because he loves stories.

I recorded another storytelling session with Uncle Oscar at my mother's house in late summer 1998 to see if any of the storytelling features I observed the first time had changed or if there was something I had missed. Oscar and my father were telling new stories and framing them as they did the traditional ones with commentary, anecdotes, prior texts, and the Kiowa social context. They were taking prior texts and embedding them into normal conversation so that it was difficult to hear where one narrative element left off and the other began. Just as they had before, the two of them were telling stories in the midst of conversation. They incorporated jokes and humorous accounts into their talk. Once again I recorded the entire session and let the storytelling develop on its own. Again, what I wanted was to explore storytelling as it really takes place. Both Kiowa storytellers and their listeners comment on stories and make interpretations as they go along (Lassiter 2000, Lawless 1992, Tedlock 1991). Although the storytelling sessions are always open and the listener may participate any time, the storyteller generally sets the tone and frames the entire event. As soon as one storyteller concludes, another can automatically begin, and so on around the circle of participant-listeners. In one setting I remember there were as many as a dozen men, three of whom told stories. The rest sat and listened and interjected comments. That session was held at the Kiowa Elders Center just before the noon meal. A museum meeting had been scheduled that afternoon, and the building buzzed like a beehive. The storytelling group, which comprised relatives and friends, collected in the same corner where John Tofpi, Wilbur Kodaseet, and Cornelius Spottedhorse, and I always sat. Many of the stories were jokes about brothers-in-law, cousins, and other close relatives. The session was an unplanned event, but like most storytelling sessions it entertained and created a warm Kiowa atmosphere.

Now, at my mother's house, while Uncle Oscar stopped to smoke, my father picked up the conversation. He started by making some comments about Kiowa children, about how they behave nowadays. I believe he was wondering why they aren't like they used to be. One of his pet peeves is that young people do not uphold their Kiowa traditions. These include speaking Kiowa, singing, dancing, and generally behaving respectfully in the good old Kiowa way. This was the general gist of his conversation.

"They have their own ways," said my father. "Maybe they like to sing that way. Some dance different."

He'd always been adamant about everybody in our family doing what we should as Kiowas. Back then there were fewer things to disagree about, and he and older members in our family dominated the talk. Nowadays, things are changing for Kiowa families, even how parents feel about the old ways. Yes, they would all like their children to stay close to home and be good Kiowas, but they also accept the fact that there are no jobs or opportunities for families in the Kiowa community. In order to make a decent living, many young Kiowas must leave home. They are mobile and leave sooner and in larger numbers than they did a generation ago. Many are better off going away. Change is inevitable. And it is this general tone one hears in Kiowa country. Many Kiowas I came in contact with while conducting interviews have accepted the changes and seem to have a good outlook on life even though it has been very difficult.

Uncle Oscar now resumed talking, mostly in Kiowa, and I thrilled at the sound. He was certainly in command of the language. I felt privileged to be there, could actually feel the warmth growing up among us by the minute. It grew and spread out. It was truly the Kiowa way of getting close to family.

"Hàu," Uncle Oscar said, "you and your wife will be by yourselves when your children grow up." We were talking about husbands and wives. He had lost his wife about a half a dozen years ago, and his daughter Tommie and her husband were now living with him, but he was still lonely, he said. He said you never get over the companionship you once had.

"Yes. I know it," I replied.

"How about them Kiowas these days?" Oscar asked, changing the subject. "Kiowa children are no good anymore."

"I know it," I responded.

He said it saddened him that, in spite of how well the parents had raised their children, many of them had not turned out very honorably.

"They had lots of kids," he said about one family we all knew. "But none of them turned out good. Yeah, they were good parents. Did everything."

In that family, only one son out of five was alive today. The others had died tragically of alcoholism. It disappointed Oscar, as it would any Kiowa elder. Kiowa families don't often talk about the sad state of affairs, but when they do it is as if the blackest cloud had descended on the land. It is an honestly deep emotional experience. During my fieldwork I had no choice but to hear out a sad and disappointed parent or grandparent.

"It's no good," my mother lamented, speaking up for the first time since we got under way. "It's happening to lots of families these days. Drinking."

She mentioned that the youngest daughter in our extended family, who had taken over the house after her mother died, threw the rest of her siblings out because they had become too unruly for her.

"I don't blame her. It's no good," said my mother. "I don't know what the world's coming to."

I asked where the oldest sister was these days. I remember seeing her around the tribal office. Not once had I realized how much trouble that family was going through. Even when you're working closely with people out there, you overlook problems or are too immersed in the present affairs to pay any attention. Could I have made any difference? Would I have tried to help or prevent some of the difficulties? It's hard to say.

Chapter VII ◎ Old Texts into New Texts

"She's the youngest one, you know," my mother said. "The oldest one left."

Uncle Oscar said the oldest lives south of Carnegie. "She's a relative, you know. She married a well-to-do Kiowa boy," he explained. "All she does is be a housewife. She just lives there. She doesn't have to work." He was obviously very happy she had met with good fortune. She'd previously been married, but when that marriage had dissolved the family was left almost destitute.

After he mentioned who had married her, we all felt better. It's good for a Kiowa daughter to meet a good man. Kiowas like good husbands for their daughters. If a woman is taken care of, that's the best thing. As my fieldwork progressed I noticed that many Kiowas talked about their children. They wanted their children to have good jobs and to be able to eat well and live in good homes. Like everybody, Kiowas are always happy to see their children profit and get ahead, but they mostly want them to be good and honorable people.

"You got it made," Uncle Oscar had told the oldest sister. "She cusses a lot," he reminded us, and then he turned back into the story and picked up the dialogue he had had with her. "Don't talk like a white man or he'll have to throw you out of the house." He was referring to curse words. Kiowa has none. If you curse at all you have to resort to English, and so he was admonishing her about her propensity for the use of foul language. We all laughed. He was adding humor to the story. I was relieved. I'd begun to think everything we were going to talk about was going to be sad. And it didn't take long to get back on a humorous track. No matter how serious a story might be, it doesn't take long for a Kiowa to mention something funny or make up a joke and in so doing let the air out of deep talk, so to speak. It is one of the ways people manage life, I imagine. A way of getting by. Uncle Oscar praised the oldest sister's good fortune and went on to tell us about the Kiowa land she and her new husband had inherited. At this point, all three of them—my mother, father, and Oscar—took up the subject of Kiowa land and how important it was for Kiowa families. Oscar talked at length about the land and who lived on it around Carnegie. But then, he brought the subject back around to the oldest sister once more. Her husband "don't talk much," Oscar had observed. "He's a good provider. He got a good running car. Got good clothing. Got good something to eat." Waggishly, he had warned the woman: "You'll ruin everything yourself. He will chase you off if you do something."

We laughed as he talked. He reminded me of Séndé. In my mind's eye I could see Séndé-Oscar sitting in front of fire telling a story to his human and animal friends. We were his audience; he was the storyteller of old. And we didn't know whether the stories were about real events or invented ones.

"Say, nephew," Uncle Oscar nudged me in the ribs suddenly. "Get me that ashtray. *Àn dé há:bòp* [I'm wanting to be smoking]."

"Hàu." I jumped up and fetched it. His Kiowa name is Tábáêl (Big Smoke). I don't know where he got that name, but it fits him perfectly.

"Yeah, she was fortunate," he went on. "God had pity on you for sure, I told her."

Oscar characteristically had opened his story with what Greg Sarris (1993) called the "vast territory that is oral" (p. 41). And in so doing was not only extending the territory but also letting the territory "be talked about and explored." Storytelling inevitably was being framed by the social context and commentary. A generous amount of interpersonal and intercultural discourse took place among participants. What now interests scholars of oral literatures, as Sarris observes, are "the broader contexts in which these literatures live" (p. 39). In other words, scholars are considering what lies beyond the spoken word, beyond their own perceptual range as listeners and readers. They are examining what that larger context says about their position as literate speakers and writers. What they include is the vast territory inherent in Native American literatures, what happens naturally and almost effortlessly in oral literature, as it does in serious literature. With Indians, at least with the Kiowas, listeners are almost always being invited to participate in the storytelling itself, to add to, to comment, to interpret, and to keep the story going. They may introduce their own stories. The storytelling frame allows this kind of discourse to occur. That is a unique feature in oral storytelling among Indians: one story is everybody's story.

Chapter VII ◎ Old Texts into New Texts

I enjoyed the subject of Kiowa families during this session. But what I found most compelling was how Uncle Oscar recounted what he had told the Kiowa girl who had come into good fortune. I had heard storytellers do this, but here it seemed all the more informative if not entertaining. He used his own tone of voice so that we were almost convinced that we were hearing him speak to her. Storytellers of great skill can affect realism with such ease that it is always a pleasure to hear them tell their stories. While Oscar talked I couldn't help thinking that I was in the presence of a great Kiowa storyteller.

After we took a short coffee break my father began a story about one of his cousins. Just like Oscar's story, this one was about someone in the immediate family. He started by telling us about B., an old Kiowa storyteller who used to visit at my grandfather's house. Dad opened his story by framing it with details we already knew. The old man would stay over a few nights sometimes at their home when he was a boy, he said, and his father would tell them after the old man left that "he was windy but good company." In other words, the old man was a good storyteller. "That whole family's like that," my father said his father would say. Now we were ready for him to tell about his chance encounter with his cousin H., who was the grandson of B. What he wanted us to know was that H. was very much like his grandfather B. and that the story would perhaps illustrate this.

I ventured down there. Down yonder, down over to that tribal complex to eat. And I got my tray of food and wondered, now where shall I sit down? [I spied cousin H. who was sitting nearby.] "Hello there, brother," I said. He raised up his head, you know. And he started right in talking real loud. And everybody in there was looking at us. They must have thought we were arguing or something. He was talking so hard. And then he started in telling me. . . . He said, "I know you like to sometimes go to the peyote meetings and things. You believe that way, and it's good. Me, I believe in this Táimê [religion]." He wants to have that. . . . "Hell, you never did go into the sun dance or Táimê," I said. "What do you know about it? You don't know anymore about it than I do. And I don't know nothing about it." That's what he was telling me over there. That's what he said. He said, "I'm going to have it right there [at my home].

No matter if I do it by myself." You know as well as I do, nobody does a sun dance by themselves. How can you honestly figure out something like that?

My father's story was meant to provoke laughter and ridicule. No Kiowa anywhere in the history of time has ever conducted the ritual sun dance alone. And this is why it is a joke story. My father told it in Kiowa, and it is more effective in Kiowa than in English. Stories, told jokingly about relatives, almost always require the listeners to be close relatives because they know the character in the story and will be amused by hearing what he did. Stories generally revolve around relatives who do stupid or odd things. The stories point out how improperly they have acted. So my father told this story. H. sometimes does say and do strange things, and his name and his shenanigans have previously been discussed among our Kiowa relatives. These stories almost always provoke laughter and humorous remarks, and in the end the listener usually agrees with the storyteller that the dubious actions perpetrated by someone like H. are almost always ridiculous in the Kiowa world.

Along these same lines, a few years ago, a Kiowa woman tried to conduct a sun dance too. She reportedly went up north and hired a Crow or Northern Cheyenne to help officiate. That was her first mistake. The other mistake she made was that she was a woman and not even in the hereditary sun dance family. Everything she had dreamed up was so anti-Kiowa that everybody in the tribe was appalled. Angry voices rose up like storm clouds all over Kiowa country. There were news releases, interviews, and all sorts of controversy. At a meeting I kiddingly mentioned a possible lynching and was soundly reproved by one of the woman's relatives. Some Kiowa elders convened to discuss what to do. In the end they tried to put a stop to the sun dance, but the woman threatened to file a suit claiming interference with her constitutional right to freedom of religion. She also charged that the elders were discriminating against her because she was a woman. There were a lot of angry words and hurt feelings among Kiowas that summer. But in the end there was no sun dance. A cloud of disappointment, which has not quite dissipated yet, hung over many Kiowas. The Kiowa sun dance was last held in 1888. There had been some talk over the years about reviving it, but nobody had gone this far. What this woman was doing was not only bold but also unbecoming a Kiowa woman, according to some Kiowas. That affair provided context for my father's story about his cousin H. Kiowas will often go back a good many years and pick up a theme or idea and recontextualize it into a current account, often in a humorous way, to make a point. That is what my father did.

When I asked my father later why he thought H. wanted to revive the sun dance, he said H. meant well but had no real sense of the sacred rite involved. "Not just anybody can conduct that sacred a ceremony by themselves. It's really very impossible to! People have the right frame of mind about it and heart, but it's very complicated."

Like many older Kiowas, my father does not hesitate to express his feelings and thoughts about fellow Kiowas. Kiowa elders are respected for their outspokenness. Wise, and having lived many years as Kiowas, they are given license to speak out on issues affecting Kiowas overall. Going outside what is considered proper will bring out their harsh criticism. If the offender is related to an elder, he will provoke harsher criticism and ridicule too.

"I wonder why he thought he could do that?" I probed further. I'd been thinking about the sun dance for a long time. It was the great medicine dance of the Kiowas. It was held every summer. And only during the sun dance was Táimê, the ritual medicine, exposed to view. Kiowas can revive it if they really want to. Perhaps one day they will.

"People do all kinds of things," my father said. "It ain't right. But they try to do it anyway."

Yes. The idea that an individual could revive the sun dance was ridiculous from the beginning. Kiowas do things collectively. As a tribe. As a people. A person who attempts to conduct a sacred service without community support is probably either brash or insincere and will, like the young woman or H., provoke anger or derision. Most Kiowas hate having any of their relatives create a situation that lets people make fun of them, and so they will often try to quash actions or behavior likely to arouse criticism by means of a joke or a story. It seems that they are, by telling a story that exposes a perpetrator or would-be perpetrator of a bad deed, letting other Kiowas know how they feel. "We have to show that this is not the Kiowa way," one Kiowa put it when the sun dance revival controversy stirred the community.

Now Uncle Oscar told the story of the bridge-naming ceremony that had occurred recently. This was the same incident Cornelius had briefly referred to. Like most people in the tribe, Oscar considered Sétáfètjàu, the ghost dance leader for whom the bridge was renamed, nobody special, only the son of a Mexican captive. In Oscar's eyes Sétáfètjàu was no real Kiowa, and he couldn't figure out why the bridge namers would choose him instead of an illustrious Kiowa to commemorate. Oscar told the story mostly in Kiowa.

"You know, over here, out west of town," he began.

Over there where White Fox lives, where people go driving, they're building a bridge . . . and so P. came over and said: "Brother, I came for something." He said that. And "Yes," I said. "You came after something?" And he said, "Over there where they're building a bridge." He said, "I'd like to dedicate it. To this here man Afraid-of-Bears," he said. And I said, "Do you know who he is?" "Well, I don't know him," he said. "Then why are you doing it?" I said. "He's a Mexican. He's a Mexican. Yeah. He's a Mexican man. Like Parker McKenzie. He's one of those," I said. "If you're going to dedicate that bridge. . . . you should know somebody. You know old man Little Bead Boy. You know White Fox. You know Louie Toyebo. That bunch," I said. "That's the ones to memorialize. That way you memorialize them, you know. Where they live way back there, you know." But this one, Afraid-of-Bears! "Over here where they used to hold the sun dance—were you there?" he asked me. "I used to help Grandpa set up camp but I don't remember exactly where," I told him. "I didn't have the foggiest notion about anything back then," I said. I never was inside [the sun dance lodge]. And I never was close there. "Let's dedicate it to Afraid-of-Bears somehow," he said. And I said, "Hell, I don't know him. Afraid-of-Bears was a Mexican! He ain't no Kiowa!" Yeah, now like if they were building this bridge over here—dedicate it to your father-in-law. So you can talk about him. What kind of a man he was. That's good, you know. People knew him. But this Afraid-of-Bears—hell, nobody knew him, you know. Yeah, he's just a little bitty fellow. He was a Mexican. Like Parker McKenzie. Like Parker McKen-

Chapter VII ◎ Old Texts into New Texts

zie's grandpa Martinez. [Oscar gestured with his hands to show how tall he was.] He was about this big! Yeah, those are the ones. Them captives. They [the Kiowas] swapped them off to each others. The Comanches and Kiowas. They got them as hired hands. They trained them. Ones like that. What you want for him? Whiskey? Yeah, they traded for whiskey too. They traded for anything.

This was one of the funniest accounts we'd heard all day, and we laughed a great deal about it. In typical Kiowa fashion, Oscar told the story several times to make sure we knew exactly what he was talking about. To make sure we knew exactly how it happened. Each time he told the narrative it was slightly different. The main point he wanted to emphasize was how stupid it was for Kiowas to name a bridge after a Kiowa nobody. Few Kiowas knew Afraid-Of-Bears. He was no leader of any measurable worth. One thing that Oscar wanted us to remember was that if you, a Kiowa, try to do something like name a bridge after someone in the tribe make sure it is a person whom all, or most, Kiowas recognize as worthy. Doing otherwise will provoke ridicule. This is a Kiowa lesson: to refrain from doing stupid things because people will make fun of you.

Somehow or another we got on the topic of Mexicans who lived with Kiowas. I asked Uncle Oscar to explain. He laughed.

"It's true," he said. "They lived with us. You could trade anything for a Mexican."

I wasn't shocked because I had heard these kinds of remarks many times in the family. As far as our family was concerned, Mexican hired hands were like members of the family. You could talk about them. Make fun of them. I'm sure they made fun back. There were many tales about so-and-so living with the Daugomah family, the Tsoodle family, and so forth. It was great fun to talk about these Mexicans. Anecdotes, gossip, tall tales abounded, grew up like wild weeds.

"They traded for them Mexicans," Oscar laughed. "Them Kiowas. Anything. You could trade for anything back then. You get them for hired hand. The Comanches got them for anything. Yeah. They trade. At Zóltò [Stinking Creek], your grandpa had one. My aunts got cross with us if we spoke to the hired hands around the house. They didn't want us to say anything out of the way to them, or be teasing them. Leave them alone, they used to tell us. *Àn bét áu:dèp* [The aunts were mean]. But we knew how to talk to them. We had our own ways of talking to each other. We talked to them when nobody was watching."

"They had their own way of talking to each other," my father said. Apparently, the Tenadooah aunts didn't want the Tenadooah boys to bother the Mexicans. They thought they were making fun of them perhaps. But, as Oscar put it, the boys and the Mexicans had ways of communicating with one another. They understood each other is what he meant.

"They hired them to cut wood, carry water," Oscar continued. "They do just about everything. They kept them. They traded for them with the Comanches. They came this way to us."

While we were talking my father mentioned Àndàlé, the infamous Mexican Kiowa captive who got on the Kiowa rolls and inherited land just like any Kiowa. He was foolish and selected the worst land around. His allotment, which was located south of Verden, turned out to be all sandstone.

My mother laughed. She hadn't said very much all morning, and I was glad she was joining in. She said she grew up when there were lots of Mexican hired hands in Kiowa homes and remembered Àndàlé well. Her parents had kept him for many years. She obviously knew lots of stories about him. I'd heard his name around the house when I was growing up. My grandparents were quite fond of him. It is said they treated Àndàlé like a son.[1]

"His lands were utterly worthless," declared my mother. Without saying it she was implying that Àndàlé was such a fool he didn't even know the difference between good and bad land. He was the kind of unlucky person Leo Rosen (1982) might describe as a schlemiel. Àndàlé might be someone who, as Rosen writes, "falls on his back and breaks his nose" (p. 286).

"Àndàlé was allotted two quarters of land that consisted almost entirely of sandrock," my mother laughed. "Sandrock. All of it was sandrock."

She was speaking Kiowa, and her remarks were funnier than if she'd been speaking in English. The Kiowa words carry suggestions, associations, and connotations other Kiowa speakers understand, and it's hard to get the same effect in English. We got a good laugh out of her small contribution. Without even trying my mother was a superb Kiowa storyteller. She had heard many humorous stories about Kiowas from her parents and relatives. One account that her mother told her she recounted to me partly in Kiowa. It's the multiplicity of voices and points of view—my mother telling what her mother said that her husband, my mother's father, told her about his sister telling him—that distinguishes it as a Kiowa tale; my mother's father was making fun of his sister for exaggerating Ábòà's charms. Remember that the narrator is my mother, whose parents are speaking.

1   They were dancing, she [mother] said.

2   Those young men were dancing.

3   They were Blackleggings[2] dancing, she said.

4   [Aunt Abbie] was bragging about her brother-in-law Ábòà.

5   They were dancing. They proceeded in the opposite direction and their hair was looooong, flowing down their backs.

6   [So Abbie] was telling my dad.

7   She was bragging about her brother-in-law dancing. Nà:hó's brother.

8   Dad helped [her] make up the story. He said: "You're bothering me!

9   [He mimicked her, saying] They were dancing and they were soooo tall and soooo good-looking."

10   They were young men and warriors and beautiful.

11   Who's your brother-in-law? [Dad said]

12   Your son!

After we finished our storytelling session, I drove home thinking about our visit at my mother's house. I had recorded the entire session, which lasted four to five hours. Next time I wanted to see if I could get my mother to record more stories and have her add some commentary about the accounts.

Chapter VIII

A Collaborative Ethnography

After my visit with Uncle Oscar and my parents, I also wanted to see if other Kiowa storytellers told stories similarly, and so I contacted Carole Willis, who is another member of the Tenadooah family. Like mom, Carole loves to tell humorous family stories to relatives in small, intimate gatherings. She is my cousin, the granddaughter of the late John and Winnie Eagleheart Tapedo of Carnegie. She grew up hearing Kiowa spoken daily. When I called her and asked if she would participate in my field study of Kiowa storytelling, she agreed instantly. She and I grew up in the same community, knew all our relatives, especially the old ones, and remember many wonderful times when they were all alive and we visited each other's homes and spent many hours telling stories and laughing. The day we met, I recorded our conversation about those good times.

"I always knew you should do a family memoir with our family," she replied happily when I told her I had been recording contemporary stories with some of our relatives for my book. We had worked together some years earlier when she was the director of the Indian education program in the Oklahoma City public schools. Not only is she knowledgeable about educational matters regarding young Indians everywhere, she is also a fluent Kiowa speaker. I find the two of us speaking more and more Kiowa every time we meet, and this time she was animated and warm, full of Kiowa expressions and joy.

Chapter VIII ◎ A Collaborative Ethnography

After we talked awhile about the Tenadooahs and storytelling, she told me a story about one of our grandpas, John Oliver (J.O.), who was my grandfather's younger brother and someone I loved very much.

"You remember that old arbor back home?"

"It was the one where we all used to gather and eat and visit. It was the best-looking arbor around."

"My grandpa had it built. It had a sidewalk leading up to it. There was a cooking facility attached to it just like the willow arbors used to have. You remember them?"

"It was huge. And cool to sit in. I remember late night visits and feasts in the summer. You all practically lived in it all summer."

"I know it. We could all sit around and even sleep in there. We did live in there all summer like a lot of Kiowas did back then. Everybody had an arbor. The bigger the better. Well, one time we were all gathered out there with grandpa J.O. and he was talking about how "jelly bean" somebody looked in a school program presented by girls. Every time I see my folks they're just jelly bean, he laughed. He was always saying that."

Jelly bean was an expression J.O. liked to use to describe someone who dressed flashily and looked sharp. Carole thought it was so funny when he expressed the term in Kiowa, and that was the beauty of that story.

"You know we learned a lot from them, didn't we?"

Carole laughed. "We sure did. Dang, it was our schooling."

"Oh, by the way, when I was talking to John Tofpi, we got onto the subject of Cedar Dale Country School and he told me he went there when he was a boy. He went to Cedar Dale before he went to Carnegie. Isn't that amazing? I didn't know that country school was that old."

Almost every one of our relatives at one time or another walked those narrow wooden halls that led to that one huge classroom where thirty or more children of all ages gathered each school day until it closed down in the early 1960s. Carole mentioned that the property on which Cedar Dale was built was donated to the state and the county by John Eagleheart Topaum who had married the second Tenadooah sister. "His vision was that his children and descendants would receive a good education," Carole volunteered.

My cousins and I drove one another crazy teasing each other about Cedar Dale School. It was a kind of embarrassment to go there. I never attended it, but many of my Tenadooah cousins did. I remember the times we would drive up into that driveway on the school bus from town to turn around and how everybody would duck behind a bush or around the corner of the schoolhouse so they wouldn't be seen and teased.

"Yeah, I went there too," Carole boasted, as if it was a privilege reserved for the very special.

I laughed and told her lots of our family went to school there.

"You can say that again. It was rebuilt in 1928, after it was destroyed by that tornado around 1927 or so."

My grandfather told a story about that tornado. It had apparently destroyed many Indian homes and killed the wife of an important medicine man, Lonebear. Lonebear and my grandfather had had some kind of disagreement.[1] "In my dreams he chased me," my grandfather said. "Even under the water. I couldn't get away from him. He was *zélbé* [endowed with extraordinary powers]. Powerful. He had his power in that single braid he wore behind his head. Storm ripped it off him and destroyed his house. It killed his wife too. Ø hôl [It killed her]. That Storm Spirit told me in my dream: Look at that man there, *ø jó:gá*. I saw him sitting there. He was looking the other way. The Storm Spirit went behind him. I'm going to show you what I can do, the Storm Spirit [said]: I'm going to take everything away from him. And it did. It even took his medicine from behind his head. That single braid of his. It ripped it off like a piece of paper."

He had told me one of those dream stories just as John Tofpi had. Grandpa loved telling these kinds of stories. Many of his stories were about magical or supernatural events and encounters between people and animals and objects. When I asked him why these things happened, he would mostly say that was how things were. Because I was so young I was often a little afraid, but I always pretended that I wasn't. I liked to ask him questions about these unnatural occurrences because they interested me, but I believe he would tell me only what he thought I could understand. The rest he left up to my imagination. And so when Carole told me about the 1927 tornado that devastated that part of the country, Grandpa's story about old Lonebear came to mind. It seems pretty well established right now that Kiowas tell stories about events, places, and people that hold their interest and become a part of the collective Kiowa consciousness. Kiowas never forget the stories because they are a part of their tribal memory and remind tribal members what it is to be Kiowa. The stories also instruct. They tell Kiowas what is good or bad, right or wrong. Of course it is necessary to remember the consequences of wrong-doing and evil. To choose the wrong action or say the wrong words can be a person's undoing. Grandpa, as long as he lived and breathed, kept my imagination alive with stories of the Kiowa way of life.

"Yeah, that storm was devastating," Carole reminded me. "It ruined lots of Kiowa homes around here."

"Tenadooah Academy," I laughed.

We reminisced about the old school and its part in our lives. She thought it had done the family good. It had helped to keep the children focused on education and a changing world. We talked about some of our cousins and how they had fared since that time. Most of the old home places are nowhere to be seen. If you drive by the sites you can sometimes see remnants of houses, a few standing brick chimneys, slabs of concrete or the dome of a cellar half buried in tall johnson grass. Sometimes the posts of old barbwire fences stick up in the sky like the bleached bones of some prehistoric animal.

"They had allotments around there," I said. "Rather than attend the public school in town, a lot of our cousins went to Cedar Dale. There was this kind of joke about Cedar Dale."

"You can say that again. We were just teasing though."

"Yeah. I know. We all made fun of that country school, but it was the central educational institution out there in the 1930s, 1940s, 1950s, and the early 1960s, when it was inactivated. One of my cousins, Calvin, never got out of the eighth grade. He wasn't too bright, as I recall. He attended, I believe, about twelve years, repeating some of the same grades because they didn't know what else to do with him. He would sometimes tell us about his lessons and the old schoolteacher he didn't get along with. I don't know where they dug her up, but she taught at Cedar Dale for many years. Somebody said she just shriveled up and blew away."

After Carole and I finished talking and decided which day we would meet again, I made a mental note to ask her to tell more stories about Cedar Dale. Because that school played such a major part in the lives of the Tenadooah family, I wanted to be sure we covered it as thoroughly as we could. I wanted to see how many different stories she knew. As always, I wanted to see what patterns there were in our family storytelling. I wanted to see how we recontextualized the stories from previous experiences. I wanted to know what social conditions informed our stories and how tribal context informed us about our own Kiowa-ness.

In the stories I recorded with John Tofpi, I'd detected some recontextualization of characters and themes into new contexts. He'd taken some characters out of some old Kiowa stories, prior texts, and embedded them into contemporary ones. Recontextualizing characters from old sources into the new was what M. Bakhtin (1981) termed *chronotope*. It is a space-time term he borrowed from mathematics, which, he notes, "expresses the inseparability of space and time. . . . We understand the chronotope as a formally constitutive category of literature" (p. 84). What his theory attempts to do in literature is to take "widely disparate periods of time" and put them together in a time realm of story. Chronotope can include characters, dialogue, and other features. We can, for example, take a character like Séndé and put him into the middle of any contemporary story if we like, and that is utilizing the chronotope.

On my later visits with Carole, we talked some about people we knew back home who exemplified some character traits of the trickster. "So-and-so is like Séndé," we would say. What it really came down to was that our grandpas were telling trickster stories all along, even before the literary establishment invented a name for what they were doing.

What I have tried to do in the past chapters is draw some conclusions about how Kiowas tell stories. Among the storytelling features that emerge are the frames that enclose the text. These frames include the so-cial or tribal context, without which Kiowa storytelling could not occur. Others are the frames that open and close stories. Kiowas tell stories in the midst of ordinary conversation without warning. These stories occur so unexpectedly that it is sometimes hard to know where a story be-gins or ends, it is so much a part of everyday conversation. It is dif-ficult to tell if what's going on in the stories is true or not. There are often unusual things happening. Sometimes one finds dreamlike people, creatures, and animals making the stories fantastic or magical creations. There are stories that open and remain open so the listener is able to interact with the storyteller by adding comments, asides, stories, inter-pretations, or other responses or remarks that make the story grow. Stories are usually told in small, intimate groups made up of relatives and close friends.

Finally, Kiowa oral storytelling, indeed all oral storytelling that takes place in this country, is nothing less than genuine American literature. Kiowa or not, any literature produced in the Americas is certainly re-markable and important in its own right. And American literature is in-complete without it. I believe the question of whether these literatures deserve serious attention has already been asked and answered to some extent here and elsewhere. The emergence of American Indian literature in this part of the world could very well be one of the most significant literary events in these times.

When I visit with Carole Willis the final time, she tells me a little more about her own family background. She tells me how surprised she is to be able to speak Kiowa. Like me, she has lived away from her Kiowa family and community for a good number of years. Many Kiowas who have moved out of Kiowa country have all but completely lost the Kiowa language.

"When two young Kiowas meet these days," I say, "it is almost certain they will not be communicating in Kiowa."

Carole agrees and says that Kiowa may very well be no more. Then sud-denly she remembers a story that her friend Sally told her, and she wants to tell me as well as she can in Kiowa. It is a humorous account about Sally, the wife of O., a person we both know well.

1   All our children came over.
2   We ate and went outside.
3   They began to play ball and were having a wonderful time.
4   How they began to play volleyball! And I envied them.
5   I joined the game and tried to jump and play like they did.
6   The following morning when I tried to get out of bed I experienced great bodily pain and difficulty!

The punch line is not in the content itself. It resides in the language. It is the way Sally put it in Kiowa that is humorous, especially the part about trying to get out of bed. The humor is in saying *tâ:bà:àu:dèp* (rise up on your feet, and difficulty to do it). Struggling to get out of bed brings to mind someone who is very old or infirm, someone who can barely manage to sit up. An elderly Kiowa might say this to explain his own physical condition, and I am sure every Kiowa can remember either a grandmother or grandfather making such a remark. That a vigorous young person like O.'s wife, Sally, should employ that expression in self-description is so funny that every time the listeners think about it they have a good laugh. The story conjures up the image of a grandmother and the incredibly funny way old folks say things in the company of their grandchildren. Kiowas who hear the story will certainly laugh.

Chapter IX

Last Words

One day I got to thinking about John Tofpi's dream story again. As time drew on I was getting bolder about asking him and the rest of my consultants storytelling questions, and they in turn were becoming more and more talkative. I believe they were beginning to see what I was trying to do, and I think they wanted to help me. I appreciated their concern and know that without these wonderful and informative Kiowas I wouldn't have gotten anywhere. So far, everything was coming along well, and I was making voluminous notes and reading many related articles and books about the oral storytelling genre. I was reading Richard Bauman quite a bit, as I was Keith Basso. But there were many other helpful works, and I was going back and forth from recordings, interviews, chit-chat, and storytelling, back to the published material. It was exhilarating to try to make meaningful connections, and I was feeling more self-assured as time went along. So I thought I might ask John to tell me his fascinating dream story again.

As I have pointed out, at first I couldn't tell if he had dreamed the story or if it was a real incident. This time he sort of rambled on about the dream again, and I didn't want to interrupt him by asking if he'd had a dream and then walked down to the bridge to locate that tree and pray as he said he had. I thought: What on earth would he be doing way down there next to the creek by our house praying anyway? And why should it matter that he saw my son and me walking on the road close by? There is nothing particularly Kiowa about that. He simply enjoyed being out there near a place where he grew up. This must have put him in that prayerful state of mind. Being there could make his dream meaningful. Maybe he concentrated better that way. But I could not ask. John T. simply thought once and for all that when he told me the dream I'd understand everything because that's how things were. That was being Kiowa as far as he was concerned. He did not feel a need to explain because we were Kiowas and Kiowas often tell personal narratives that undoubtedly belong to some realm of human understanding only Kiowas are supposed to understand. As ordinary as sitting down, talking, standing up, and walking, so is going somewhere away from your house to pray or think or whatever. My grandfather would get up early in the mornings and walk out by the creek to pray. I would lie awake listening to him going, going. Out there on the creek bank. His voice would go out over the land, as far away as anybody could imagine, to confront the known or unknown, perhaps the inscrutable. Yes, that was it. To know yet not know. That was an important question to ask one's self. Did John Tofpi not say so in his dream? That the tree "looked like an outstretched hand," in an attitude of supplication. Did he not even show me how it looked by extending his own hand outwardly and cupped? "Like that," he had said. That done, he had looked at me a long time as if searching for a sign of recognition. A recognition of what? To get my reaction, I imagine. No doubt about it, in his own mind he had been witness to a kind of miracle, and I think he wanted me to show some appreciation for it.

"See?" John T. went on as if to reenforce what he'd told me several times already. "Just like that it looked." Like any good Kiowa, he was equating that dream to a vision of something real and true.

My Kiowa storytelling consultant looked at me and studied me over for a long time and then he said, "It was something, huh?"

"Yeah," I replied. "It sure was."

What else was I supposed to say? He expected me to respond and I did. I could tell he wanted me to know that this was no imaginary happening or fluke, but a real incident. He wanted to be absolutely sure that I knew

Chapter IX ◎ Last Words

where he stood on this important matter of the dream. I'd heard Kiowas tell stories when I was growing up, stories too important and meaningful to let go. You had to be certain that whoever heard your story knew exactly how it occurred and how it affected you. That's what was important. As far as John was concerned, or any good Kiowa storyteller, for that matter, you had to tell the whole story, which meant your own understanding of it and commentary on it as you recounted it. And if you were a really good storyteller, you had to make sure your listener was with you all the way. You made sure by asking questions like: Is this so? Is this how it is? Yes? No? Right? This is what John Tofpi was trying to get at that afternoon sitting on the sofa at the Kiowa Elders Center when he told his dream story a second—or was it a third?—time. He was bringing me into the realm of his consciousness the good old Kiowa way. The way Kiowas are supposed to tell a story. My grandfather talked about similar revelations. I've heard him tell what he'd seen in his dream and how it equated with this or that in real life, and you didn't know where one part of the story left off and another part started up again.

Epilogue

You imagine that I am here in this room, do you not? That is worth
something. You see, I have existence, whole being, in your imagination. It is but
one kind of being, to be sure, but it is perhaps the best of all kinds. If I am
not here in this room, grandson, then surely neither are you.
—N. Scott Momaday, 1970

Difficulty of Translations and Interpretations

For a listener from outside the tribe it can be difficult to follow a Kiowa
story and very often maddening. Elsie Clews Parsons (1929), for instance,
must have struggled a great deal trying to interpret the Kiowa narratives
she collected and published. If you read the stories closely it becomes
clear that she didn't have any real interest in magical realism, which is
one of the chief features in Kiowa storytelling. Consider the following excerpt:

My brother Hoseptai (gun walking), is a medicine man. I do not know how he
became one. I think he had a dream. He did not go to the mountain to fast.
He was asked by a White man to cure his wife. . . . (p. 7)

Nowhere does Parsons explain how the man in the story became a
medicine man. There are no subliminal encounters or voices speaking
out of the rocks or clouds. It is just a straightforward narrative. That is
the trouble with many translated texts published during the first third
of the twentieth century. In his biography, Desley Deacon (1997) tells us

114

Epilogue

that Parsons's "first interest as an anthropologist was in Pueblo Indian culture and the American Southwest" (p. 21). Her true interests were not in language or oral literatures and may account for the bad translation of the Kiowa material.

Hers was not the only work on Indian narratives during this time. C. F. Lummis came out with *Pueblo Indian Folk Stories* (1910); Franz Boas published *Kutenai Tales* (1918); Robert Lowie published *Myths and Traditions of the Crow Indians* about the same time. In 1919, William Jones published *Ojibwa Texts*, Volume 2. In 1926, George Grinnell published *By Cheyenne Campfires*, and in the following year Parsons published *Tewa Tales*, followed in 1929 by *Kiowa Tales*. Last, Ruth Benedict (1931) published *Cochiti Tales*. I suspect that, at the rate that these works were coming out, they are probably not much better than Parsons's work.

Alice Marriott published Kiowa stories that she collected in the early and mid-1940s. *Winter-telling Stories* came out in 1947 and was reprinted in 1963 as *Saynday's People*. It is a collection of Séndé stories. They are authentic, but like Parsons, Marriott takes liberties with the language and makes her own interpretations. Note the following passage:

As Saynday was coming along, he met some of the animals. There were Fox and Deer and Magpie. They were all sitting together by a prairie dog hole, talking things over. (p. 11)

In the original Kiowa story, these animals had not even met, much less spent time "talking things over." The animals just showed up at the place where the strange beings lived and were playing with the sun. One of the animals in the troupe, a fox, entered the games and *kóbéhậfè* (took away) the sun from the players. In *Saynday's People* the animals try to find some way to get the sun. These animals "think" about how they can solve their problem. In many traditional Kiowa stories, as well as other Indian stories, much action is unmotivated action. Things occur often for no apparent reason. In Marriott's story, however, we find Séndé and the animals planning or strategizing about how they will accomplish their goals. In the original Kiowa story they simply come together and then take away the sun, presumably on behalf of the Kiowas. They are not cuddly, cute animals like the kinds you find in Disneyland. These are wild animals with very sharp teeth, and they will bite humans and eat them if given the chance. They are not concerned with moral values or human behavior. Séndé and his entourage simply want light in the land and mean to get it any way they can. What drives the original Séndé narrative springs from the Kiowa collective mind working to survive in a harsh world. When one reads Marriott's translated stories, however, something Kiowa is missing. One gets something one might find in an Aesop's fable or a Grimm's fairytale: Marriott seems intent on justifying certain actions in stories.

In another passage of the same story, we hear Deer complaining to Séndé.

"We don't like the darkness," to which Saynday responds, "What's wrong with the darkness?" Deer answers, "It won't let things live and be happy." (p. 11)

I have never heard such a line in the original story. Since when did Kiowas speak of being happy or happiness? No such terms exist in Kiowa. I do not mean that Kiowas lack feelings of joy or happiness. They just don't say things like *happy* in the way some people do. Marriott puts words and sentiments into the mouths of characters, it would appear. The question is: Who benefits? Not only is Marriott taking liberties with original texts, she is also misrepresenting Kiowas. She leads readers to suppose Kiowas think and feel in ways that are uncharacteristically Kiowa.

In conclusion I want simply to say that authors have often misrepresented Indian values and Indian people. They have too often made textual and interpretive changes in purportedly accurate transcriptions. We do not want to see, as Greg Sarris (1989) points out, "the Indian . . . pushed out of the way, confined in unseen corners of the territory" (p. 27).

The stories my grandfather told me had elements of the imaginary and the real in them. I never thought back then to ask him if his stories were real because they seemed so. When he told me the tale of old man Tenadooah going up on top of Mount Sheridan and how the collared lizard that confronted him was "big as a greyhound," I believed it. He did too. The old man Tenadooah would not make up such a tale. To do such a thing would be shameful. It wasn't in his character to lie. Kiowas will ridicule such a man.

My grandfather's own story about his encounter with Spirit Man in the hospital where he lay mortally ill is such a story as his father's. It is both magical and real. Spirit Man was the incarnation perhaps of a dream or hope. He was not a physical presence in the sense that you and I are, but pure spirit, yet whole. At first my grandfather felt Spirit Man's presence in that room, and then he beheld Spirit Man standing at the foot of his bed. "Stand up and go," Spirit Man told him. And my grandfather did. He was a witness to his own miraculous recovery, and like a true Kiowa he told no one but his own family.

Storytelling has always been a source of great entertainment for all people. As a further condition for making things seem real in stories, storytellers have traditionally told stories during special times and in certain settings. It is hard to imagine one telling a heroic epic early in the morning or during work. These are not typically conducive times for any person to dream or wonder or imagine. Better a story be told in the evening, when the shadows are long and the fires are low so the listener can gaze into the flames and imagine the unimaginable.

When I asked my grandfather one time if he really believed that Táimê rose into the sky like a cloud of white smoke the last time the Kiowas performed the sun dance, he looked at me and smiled and said in Kiowa, "You think maybe so?" In his own way he was putting me in a position to inquire into a belief system. It didn't matter whether what he was telling me in the story was real or not. What really mattered was not so much that I understood the meaning of the event but that I should have a sense that something extraordinary and wonderful happened to the Kiowas long ago.

Appendix

The Coming of Táimê to the Kiowas

1. Tògàu gà dáu:mê.
2. Ó, tògàu gà dáu:mê.
3. Qácómdà áugàu gà thàumáum:déhèl:déè gà dáu:mê.
4. Hábé áuhyàu:déè jógúl ø dáu:mè:dè káuàun jógúl dáu:mê.
5. Máun hàgà ø hé:màun:dàu.
6. Hàgà jépjéhè ø dáu GÌGÁU ø káu:àunhèl GÌGÁU qáptàu ø qómó:hèldè GÀU mà:yí átà:dèàl ø qómó:hèldèè hègáu è yát:tài:dò:hèl.
7. QÀUT hègáu áuhyáudè máun é:gàu mén fítfásàtjàu.
8. Àkô hègáu égàu châu yá hê:jèhài:gàdàu:déchò dè hê:jètjàu.
9. Há:jèl táui thá:gá máun án hái:gádàu NÉ óbàhàu náu yá hê:jèhài:gàdàu.
10. À:kô, hègáu hágá gà dáu:mè:déè hègáu gà hé:màun:dè:hèl.
11. Héjáu yá:jé hègáu máun è cí:dê.
12. NÈGÁU hègáu ø kî:hèl gàu ø é:bà:hèl GÌGÁU máun háu:gàut, hàgà zêbà—háyá hàundè ø dó:cá gàu ø é:bà:hèl.
13. GÌGÁU háundé ø jó:hèl NÀU émgàu é:gàu án àundáu:mê GÀU áugáufì án àundáu:mê.
14. Buffalo àn àundáu:mê.
15. Nàu máò:dè. Hègáu máun gà dónmê, bót sái:gá àn ó ópchò àn cául háyá ét àuzó:nê NÀU èt dónmê.
16. Há:chòdèfè:dò hègáu án àundáu.

17 NÀU hègáu àunhí:hèl.

18 Hègáu gà hóljàu áuhyàudè GÀU jócà dè hí:jáu, ø áu:dê.

19 GÌGÁU ø àunhîhèl.

20 GÌGÁU ø àunhîhèl dècàugàu, háundé ø jóhèl NÈGÁU fái ø yíhèl.

21 ØYíhèldèchò gà kó:hí:hèl.

22 Hègáu ø áudê: À:kô, óihyàu gàt kómàu:gù:jàu GÀU jói à
     kóbà:thàu.

23 GÌGÁU káhí:gâu à âuià:thàu GÀU háyátjò hègáu án àundáu:thâu.

24 NÀU fòi gà âuiàunhà:fèjàu, ø áu:dê.

25 GÌGÁU jói gà ái:hyêl.

26 GÀU máun hágá è cîl:déè: ø chán.

27 GÌGÁU èm dè:máu.

28 Káhí:gáu fòi án fí:pátcáhèl GÌGÁU hègáu fègáu gà áihèl.

29 GÌGÁU áugàu kí:dél áugàu gà àunyí:gátò:dàu:dèè: ø chánhèl.

30 À:kô, hègáu áutcàu án àundáu:dégùi hègáu èm àuzónhèl.

31 GÌGÁU ø àunhîhèl.

32 Ø Àunhîhèl GÀU hègáu gà bá:hèl NÉGÁU máu:sàutjè háòdè hègáu
     án àundáu:mê.

33 NÈGÁU ø fáu:tà:hèl.

34 GÌGÁU háundé ø jó:hèl NÀU fègáu gà kó:hí:hèl.

35 Nègáu fègáu áuihyàu hègáu ø máu:gú:hèl.

36 GÀU fòi jói gà áihyèl

37 GÀU fòi èm dè:máuhèl.

38 Káhí:gáu fòi hègáu gìgáu áu:dê gà áihyèl GÀU áugàu gà
     àunmáu:gú:déè ø âuichànhèl. Némgàu fòi héjáu án àundáu:mê.

39 Hègáu ø àunhî:hèl NÀU hègáu án sáutàun:dàu:mè.

40 Tó:cà é:gàu á tó:dáu:mê NÀU ø pàidáu:mê.

41 NÈGÁU hègáu, hádàljè hègáu hâuigàu máu é hágá hègáu èt táujáu,
     ø áu:dè, dèàu:tàup.

42 NÀU fègáu é:hàudè third night.

43 Hègáu fòi gà kó:hêl.

44 GÌGÁU èm cò:dósàutjèjàu:.

45 Émgàu sáutàl á cótjé é:gàu droppings.

46 Néjáu gà á:fáu:dà:.

47 Ah! Hègáu gà kó:háu:.

48 NÈGÁU gà âuiài:hèl GÀU ó: èm dè:máu:hèl.

49 Yí:cáyàu, hègáu yí:cáyàu:déè: hègáu ø bá:hèl.

Appendix

50 Ø kápáui:déhèl NÈGÁU ø bá:hêl NAU émgàu án áubáu:à:dàu:mê
   dè:àu:tàup.

51 GÀU à:kô, fourth dayyàu gà dáu:mêdèè: hègáu ø qáu:jéhèl.

52 Hègáu ø táu:hêl.

53 Ø táu:hêl.

54 É:gàu buffalo ø àunbáu: yí:cá kì.

55 Ø táu:hêl.

56 NÈGÁU ø táu:hêl NÈGÁU áungàu ø qá:hìàum:dè:hèl.

57 Hègáu ø qá:hìàum:dè:hèl.

58 NÈGÁU ø jó:nê, "Èm á:. Èm á:. É táihì," ø jó:nê.

59 NÈGÁU ø táihì:hèl.

60 Hègáu bôt máun ø cí:tà.

61 Hàgà ø sáumtà.

62 Háyát ø dáu:cá.

63 Hègáu ø táihì:hèl NÀU qóp è éthèl:déè: hègáu ø fàu:hé:béhèl,
   qópcá.

64 GÌGÁU áuhyàu qópcá áugàu è éthèl:déè: hègáu qópfá ø
   fàu:hé:béhèl.

65 GÌGÁU áu:hàu, áuhyàu hègáu ø fàu:dó:dê.

66 GÌGÁU à:kô bétàu hègáu án màuhé:mê.

67 Bétàu án màuhé:mè, hègáu háun:dé.

68 É:gàu qáu:jó, bá jó:gà. Cúngà gà dáu:dè. Bétàu áuhyàu hègáu án
   màuhé:mê.

69 Dáu:chái:gá gà dáu:mê.

70 Dáu:chái:thàu:gà gà dáu:mê.

71 Áu:hyàudè hègáu án màu:hé:mê.

72 À:kô, hègáu máun án màuhém gàu án hái:gá.

73 NÈGÁU ø tépdàu:fêhèl NÈGÁU ø kîhèl GÌGÁU ø bá:hèl.

74 GÀU jó:cà ø chánhèl.

75 Jó:cà ø chánhèl.

76 GÌGÁU à:kô, hègáu NÈGÁU é:dè qáptàu GÀU mà:yiàl, bétàu háun
   óbâui:fòihyóm:qà:còm:qà:hì: máun è dáu:mê.

77 NÀU à:kô, hègáu ø jó:nê, "À:kô, hègáu cyói:dê máu tái:dò.

78 GÀU cyói:dê hègáu à tháu," ø jó:nê.

79 "Dè kóàu:zòn:jàu," ø jó:nê.

80 NÈGÁU qáptàu—È á:dê, tá:càu:gàu—NÀU ø jó:nê, "É:gàu jó gát
   à:sàuldéè áu:fáu: yí: hàundè gà pá:," ø jó:nê. "Bàt bó:," ø jó:nê.

121

81 "Bàt bó:," ø jó:nê.

82 "GÀU . . . bôt thá:gá ø dáu jáu GÀU ø dáu tái:dò.

83 Gát fītfáusátjàu NÀU bàt bó: éhàudè.

84 Há:gâi, há:gâi yán áu:jàu," ø jó:nê.

85 "Há:gâi yán áu:jàu," ø jó:nê.

86 NÀU hègáu é:dè, ø jó:nê:

87 "Há:gâi gà dáu:mêdè?"

88 Câudè máu gà héngùtqòdàu:mè GÀU gà sáuihé:dàu.

89 Háyát ø kóhài:dàu:cà?

90 Né yí: gà dáu:mê.

91 NÈGÁU é:dè gà cáumhèldè gà háu:hèl:dè, bétàu hègáu dáu:chái:thàu:gà gà dáu:mê:dè hègáu qáujó é:gàu, bá jó:gà.

92 Táimê.

93 *Táimê máun èm káu:thàu:yà?*

94 Qáu:jó:.

95 Áuihyàudè dáu:chái:gá bètáu gà dáu:mê.

96 Fâidàu:chài:qì ø dáu:mê.

97 Háu hègáu háiòdè èm tháu:dáu?

98 Fâidàu:chài:thàu:gà gà dáu:mê.

99 Qácómdà é:gàu gà ánmàdéè.

100 Fâigà. É:gàu fâithàu NÀU jéhàundè gà cúá:thàu:.

101 Dáumàl è sô:thàu.

102 Gà tá:dá:thàu GÀU sôn gà qíá:thàu.

103 Á:kì:gà!

104 Hát jéhàundè fruits gà qíá:thàu:dè gà dáu:mê.

105 GÀU à:kô, fâigà gà dáumê.

106 Fâikì:dà.

107 É:gàu fái:fáu:dà.

108 Qácòmdà.

109 Bètáu fâigà jéhàundè gà cúá:hèl QÀUT thá:gá gà qíá:yì:dè gà dáu:mê.

110 Fí:gá gà dáu:mè GÀU life gà dáu:mê.

111 Qácómdàdè.

112 Dáu:chái:dègà bètáu áuhyàudè gà dáu:mêdè, áuihyàudè:dè bètáu gà háu:hèl:dè ø dáumê.

113 Táí:mé gà dáu:, bá jó:gà.

114 Qáu:jó:dé áuihyàudè dáu:chái:thàu:gà gà dáu:.

Appendix

115 Fâidàu:chài:thàu:gà gà dáu:.

116 Fâikòzài:yàu hègáu jéhàundè áutcàu fruit hát gà qíá:dàu:dè.

117 Augustyàu, Septemberyàu.

118 Óihyàu gà jâyà.

119 Jé:é:!

120 Fruit.

121 Jé: fi̱:gá: bát fàutjàudè gà da̱u:mê.

122 Jédàum:tài: gà qíá:yì:dè: gà da̱u:mêdè, áuihyàu:dè
dáu:chái:thàu:gà gà da̱u:mêdè áuihyàu:dè, Ta̱imê da̱u:mêdè
áuihyàu:dè gà fàudó:dê.

123 Dáu:chái:gá:dèfè:dò é̱:gàu fâigà Cáuiqàco̱:bàu Ta̱imê á
dàu:chài:hèl, bá jáu:e̱

124 jé: ém cháthá:dê.

125 Q̱ÀUT jé: àn á ó̱:ta̱:yì:.

126 Hègáu gà bá:tháu NÀU fâigà óihyàu gà áum:déthàu.

127 Bétàu hègáu dáu:chái:gà áuihyàu ém qí:jáu:.

128 Ém qí:jáu: GÌGÁU a̱:kô, á bá:tháu.

129 GÀU óihyàu gà áum:déthàu NÈGÁU á jó:jép.

130 Jé: á jó:jépdéè̱: hègáu cáulàl háu:bè pa̱u:mà.

131 Fí:gá:àl!

132 É̱:gàu é: hát gà dáu:dè hègáu jé: gà jâyàu.

133 Zái:yâu gà da̱u:mê.

134 Fí:gá: gà da̱u:mê.

135 À̱:kô, hègáu jéhàundè fi̱:gá: gà màu:hó:tháu:déè̱:, zái:yâu gà
da̱u:mêe̱: hègáu dáu:chá:igá hègáu gà a̱umàu.

136 Hègáu Q̱áu:jó á dàu:chàtjàu.

137 Hègáu áuihyàudè ém dáu:chái:tháu:déè̱: áuhàu jé: á báu:dèthàu:
GÀU ém qú:jàu.

138 GÌGÁU dáu:chái:gá, áuhyàudè gà a̱umà.

139 Dàu:qí: bétàu Ø da̱u:mê:dè à:hô:dè â a̱u:màu.

140 Á ò̱:ta̱:dàu:chàt:jàu:dè: gà da̱u:mê.

141 Q̱áu:jó é̱:gàu ø dáu:dé.

142 À̱:kô, hègáu dáu:chái:gá áuihyàu gà dáu:déè̱: hègáu Cáuigú á
da̱u:mê.

143 GÀU Cáuigú dàu:chài:thàu:gà gát da̱umê.

144 Dáuchâi:thàu:gà gà da̱u:mê áuhyàudè.

145 Q̱áu:jó áugàu ø dáu:dè . . . Fâidàu:chài:qì ø da̱u:mê.

146   Áuhyàudè gà fàu:dó:dê.

147   *Háu hègáu háiọdè yán hái:gá?*

148   À:kô, fâidàu:chài:qì ø dáu:mê:déè: hègáu Cáu:kị, áugàu háungáu
      àn Cáuigú ó: ànqî: ém dáu:chátjàu. Dáu:chái:thàu:gà gà dáu:mê.
      Áuhyàugàu.

149   Dáu:chái:gà gà fàu:dó:dê.

150   Cáuigú áuhyàudè gà áu:hêl in the beginning.

151   Jọ́:gá, Cáuijọ̀:gà GÀU ẹ́:hàudè áugàu háundé Cáuigú Tàlyóp(gàu),
      bá jọ́:gàdè. Áuhyàugàu.

152   GÀU dáu:chái:gà.

153   Cáuigú. Áuhyàudètjò ém dáu:chái:lî:jàu.

154   Thófé:gû:dè:thàu:gà gà dáu:mê.

155   Religion gà dáu:mê.

156   *Háu châu gà kạ́:u dáu:chái:gà?*

157   Áuhyàudè Cáuigú gà thàumàu:hèldè gà dáu:mêdò dáu:chái:èl.
      Qáujó ø àum:déè:. À:kô, hègáu jéhàundè.

158   Fị́:gá:àl.

159   GÀU cáulàl.

160   Jéhàundè zái:yâu gà âumàu.

161   GÀU háu:bê jé: gà chánmàdéè:—ém ọ́:tạ́:yàiạu:màu.

162   Ém dáu:chátjàu.

163   Dáu:chái:èl gà dáu:.

164   Hègáu áu:hàu fâi:yàu á báu:dé:thàu:.

165   Xáli:chọ̀:hyòp.

166   Qọ́:báu: Ancient ones.

167   Real old.

168   Áuhyàu:gàu bét dáu:chát:jàu.

169   Sạ̀:dàu. He-yo-he! O-yo-he-yo! He-yo-he! He-yo-ho!

170   Áuihyàudè.

171   Sạ̀:dàu bét dáu:chát:jàu.

172   À:kô, ẹ́:gàu jé: á dáu:.

173   Cáuigú á dáu: GÀU hát háundé áutcàu. GÀU jê:yì:gàu:.

174   Hègáu áuihyàu jé:hàui ém dáu:chát:jàu:

175   GÀU ém gún:màu.

176   Á ọ́:dáu:.

177   Yí:cá kì.

178   Bôt jé: háundé yí:cá kì gà áumgá.

Appendix

179   Yí:cá kì ém gún:màu: GÀU ém dáu:chát:jàu.

180   Ém dáu:chát:jàu.

181   Áugàu Qáu:jóchél déè:. Bị:dàu. Áugàu á dáu:gàu yí:cá: kì. Fị:hé.
Tọ:hé ém dáu:chátjàu.

182   Qácóm:dàè.

183   E:gàu dáum è qáu:dèè.

184   Á qácòm:à:dé:thàu:gà.

185   Dáu:chái:thàu:gà gà dáu:déè:.

186   Jé:cùngà gà tháu:.

187   Jéhàundè gà tháu: áuhyàu.

188   Ául:káui:gáàl: gà tháu:.

189   Háun háundé tẹ:dádàu:màu:dè.

190   Cáuidàu:chài:èl gà dáu:.

191   NÀU bàt kóbọ.

192   Áuhyàu. É:gàu bè chát:jàu. Áuhyàudè cúnthàu:gà gà dáu:dè . . .
Éhàudèkì: héjáugú:hyàu bàt jáu:.

193   Áugàu bè gúnmàu:dè. Bôt èm háiàun:dàu: háchòdè cúngà gà
fáu:dè. NÀU áuhyàu gà fáu:hèl:dè: gà dạu:mê:dè: gà dáu:dê.
Dáu:chái:èl gà dạumê.

194   Nà:kô, hègáu Cí:thái:dáu:dè:qì: ø émhàu hít. GÀU ø zélbé bôt.
GÀU gà étfáté:thà:dàu.

195   Gà têm!

196   Áuhyàudè The Beginning gà dáu:dè gà thàumtém.

197   Dé zélbé!

198   Bàt kóbọ.

199   À:kô, áugàu á hó:nâuqàu:jò:—Kàu:jólâ:qàu:jò: á kàu:màu—
hóndàu:mè:.

200   Áuhyàudè.

201   Áuhyàudè.

202   Bétàu Qáu:jó ø hóndàu:déè: á Qáu:jócí:dê NÀU kísáukòhài gà
áumdéhèl.

203   NÀU jé:hàui á Qáu:jócí:dê GÀU gá jàu:bà.

204   "Áugàu! Áugàu háundé ø báudà! Áugàu háundé!"

205   Jé: á Qáu:jócì:dè GÀU á bọ:.

206   Áugàu Qáu:jó: ø dáu:. Áugàu gà dáu: háundédèè:. Ø báu:dèhèl
GÀU ø thái:dáu:mê.

207   GÌGÁU àu:tàup ø étáumdéhèl. GÀU ø étáumdéhèl. NÀU á

jàu:bà:hèl. NÈGÁU báu:dàhèl. GÌGÁU èm hâhèl. GÌGÁU á
jàu:bà:hèl. NÀU ø bá:hèl. GÀU ø pànbáyí:hêldè. Áuihyàu.
Áuhyàudè Ǫàu:jò:dàu:chài:gà. Cáuidàu:chài: gà dáu:dèfè:dò é:gàu
ém gúnmàu.

208   Áuhàu cúngàdè gà chándè èm áundàu:dò èm jétjàu.
209   Chólhàu. Ódèhàu.

The Mother Deer, Her Death Song

(As told to Oscar Tsoodle by his grandfather Tenadooah)

1   Ø jógà, á cîl.
2   Ø jógà.
3   Human corral á àu:mè, ø jógà.
4   É àn hábêkò àn tháp chólhàu ét hótjàu.
5   Óp háyá máun ét á:lé.
6   Nègáu táuchò ét á:lé.
7   Hègáu è káundàu.
8   Nègáu tháp án dáu:áun, ø jógà kòjè.
9   Tháp án dáu:áun, ø jógà.
10   Gìgáu ø jógà, Óp á à:lè.
11   Nègáu óp táuchò á à:lè," ø jógà.
12   Ìfé:dò ém óbáui hè:jètjàu.
13   Tháp èm dáu:vâigàu, ø jógà.
14   À tháu:dáu, ø jógà.
15   Í:dè hègáu á àlhòtbàu, ø jógà.
16   Nègáu í:dè ø á hègáu cháumà ø dáu:à, ø jógà.
17   Gìgáu èm dáu:vâigàu! ø jógà.
18   Gìgáu dáu:gá ø hâfè:
19   He-ye-ya! He-ye-ya! He-ye-ya!
20   He-ye-yo! He-ye-ye-ye!
21   Égàu hègáu ø chángá, ø jógà.
22   Gàu tháp dén á dóyà, ø jógà.
23   Nègáu á ì:jè gôm ø dáu:á.
24   Nègáu gà dáu:káum, ø jógà.
25   Hé! Bé tháu:hâl!
26   Bé tháu:hâl!

Appendix

27 Áu:dé hègáu án dáu:f<u>ó</u>:<u>à</u>!
28 <u>É</u>gàu tháp èm dáuvâigàu, ø jógà!
29 He-ye-ya! He-ye-ya! He-ye-ya!
30 He-ye-yo! He-ye-ye-ye!
31 Káun náu à hi̧thàudè!
32 À áu:lyî!
33 Í gà cí:hòlàul:yà!
34 Dáugá <u>é</u> dáu!
35 He-ye-ye-ye!
36 Èm dáu:vâigàu tháp, ø j<u>ó</u>gà.
37 Gàu gà dáu:<u>è</u>: à tháu:dáu:.

Áb<u>òà</u>

1 Ém gúnmàu, ø j<u>ó</u>:gà.
2 Jógú:dáu ém gúnmàu.
3 Ém T<u>ó</u>:k<u>ó</u>:gá:gùnmàu, ø j<u>ó</u>:gà.
4 She [Aunt Abbie] was bragging about her brother-in-law Áb<u>òà</u>.
5 Ém gúnmàu. Hègáu gáp ét gúnmàu gàu ául bé cí:nyî:.
6 She [Abbie] was telling my dad.
7 She was bragging about her brother-in-law dancing. Nà:hó's brother.
8 Dad helped [her] make up the story. He said, "Gàu ø há:bê!
9 Á xá:dè gàu á cy<u>ói</u>!"
10 Jógú:dáu è dáu: gàu è sólèdàu gàu bét dólbé.
11 Nàu hàjél ø dáu:.
12 <u>É</u>hàudé ì:!

Sally's Story as told by Carole Willis

1 Jé: s<u>â</u>:dàu dét chán.
2 Gát f<u>í</u>:pátcá gàu gúp è tép.
3 Ém pàuá:jóyài<u>à</u>u:màu gàu bét véfàu:dà.
4 Háundé <u>ó</u>:dé ét yái<u>à</u>u:màu nàu à qòmt<u>á</u>:!
5 À jò:chán gàu náuál háyáàl dè gúnmàu, s<u>â</u>:dàu áugàu én jáu:dèchò.
6 Gìgáu dè hâ:jàu, à <u>á</u>u:dèp, né <u>é</u> tâ:bà:àu:dèp!

127

Notes

Introduction

1. Many Indian tribes do give-aways. The great potlatch of the Pacific Northwest is a good case in point. Here, elaborate give-aways occur to assure tribal solidarity and wealth.

Chapter I

1. Harrington (1928).

2. The Tàlídàui is one of nine medicines the Kiowa people have in their possession. There once were ten (known as the Tàlídàui:gàu or Ten Grandmothers), but one was destroyed in a fire in the 1930s. No one knows where they came from or when, but they are among the oldest and most revered spiritual objects in the tribe. Most Kiowa elders refuse to talk about them because the medicines are too sacred to discuss.

My grandfather was a keeper of one of the medicines when I was a boy. I remember people coming to the house all the time to pray. They brought prayer offerings: shawls, blankets, quilts, fabric cuts, money, and even food. Sometimes my grandfather would accompany these people into the special room where the medicine was kept and pray for them. I was always curious about what they were praying about but kept my distance. Once, when I was very ill, I entered the room with my grandfather so he could offer a prayer on my behalf. It was as still in there as an empty cathedral or synagogue. I was somewhat afraid. But my grandfather told me it would be all right.

"You must know these things were given to our people long ago so that we could find our way through this life," he said. "Never fear these things. All of those old things that these medicines contained were removed from them long ago. Do you understand what I'm telling you?"

"Yes," I think I said, even though I didn't. There was much about the medicines that no one understood or understands today. But I was at least reassured that he knew what he was doing and that he would never put me in the presence of something that would harm me.

3. Sègâi (Uncle) Oscar died in March 1999. He was perhaps the last classical Kiowa speaker and traditionalist. I do not know anybody in the tribe who can possibly fill the empty place this great Kiowa left. He was one of my grandfather's favorite nephews. He lived only two miles from where I grew up. A complex man, Oscar Tsoodle could make you laugh with one of his witticisms and in the next instant shock you with an unpredictable off-color remark.

4. In her introduction to *Kiowa Tales*, Parsons bemoans the fact that one of her storytelling consultants was arrogant and his disposition "undoubtedly an asset for the young men in the old war days and . . . encouraged by tribal practices" (p. xi). She also notes that it is not helpful to work with the "younger generation who are either ignorant of the tribal past or ashamed of it and anxious to rationalize it into present frame of things, [for] it is these unsympathetic young people who worry both a storyteller and a recorder" (p. xi).

5. Tedlock (1983) writes: "Excluding less formal accounts of recent history and personal experience, Zuni narratives fall into two categories: Either they are a part of the *chimiky'ana'kowa* (origin story) which can be told at any time of day or in any season, or they are *telapnaawe* (tales) which are told only at night and during winter. Both kinds of narrative are set in the *inoote* (long ago) before the introduction of objects and institutions recognized as belonging to the period of European contact, but the *chimiky'ana'kowa*, which accounts for most of the major features of Zuni social organization, belongs to a period when the world was 'soft,' while the *telapnaawe* are set in a world which had already hardened, though it was still not quite like the present world. The *chimiky'ana'kowa* is regarded as literally true, even by some Zunis with Christian leanings, but *telapnaawe* are regarded as fiction."

One day as we were driving into Zuni from the east, Andrew Peynetsa began recalling a *telapnanne* he had previously told me. He pointed out the cave where *Haynawi* (a monster) had trapped a little girl in the story; several miles beyond, at Corn Mountain, he pointed out the place where the *Ahayuuta* twins (protector gods) had been living when they heard the girl's cry for help. He noted the distance between the two places and said, 'Nobody would believe they could hear here. That's just a story.'

Notes

Joseph Peynetsa expressed a similar view of *telapnaawe*: 'When you are a kid you believe them, but then you grow up and realize they couldn't have happened,' and Walter Sanchez when he was unable to think of any real parallel for the events in one of his own narratives, gave as his excuse the fact that the narrative in question was a *telapnanne*.

When a narrative is a *telapnanne* it is clearly identified as such by the formulaic frame which encloses it" (pp. 159–160).

For more information, see Tedlock (1983), ch. 5, "The Poetics of Verisimilitude."

6. Aristotle (1954), 259. The quotation is from 1460a in *The Poetics*.

7. According to Tedlock (1983): "The phenomenological poetics of Gaston Bachelard, instead of curving ever inward upon the forms of language, opens up both sides of the dialectic between what he calls the 'formal imagination,' which we may take to coincide at least partially with Jakobson's 'poetic function,' and the 'material imagination,' which in its purest form deals with 'direct images of matter' (Bachelard, *On Poetic Imagination and Reverie*, 10–11). Here I am reminded, once again, of the question Joseph Peynetsa once put to me while we were working on a Zuni story: 'Do you see it, or do you just write it down?' And as another Zuni said, taking the narrator's point of view, 'If you are really true to a story you make it like it's right in front of you.' In Zuni storytelling, then, the material imagination takes precedence over the formal imagination, and my discussions of the poetics of verisimilitude and of time in storytelling . . . have been, in effect, explorations of the material side of Zuni poetics" (p. 160).

8. By and large, great literary scholarship is constructed on Greek models, presumably because the Greeks had invented a writing system for their language. Ong (1992) contends that by Plato's day (427?—347BC) "a change had set in: the Greeks had at long last effectively interiorized writing—something which took several centuries after the development of the Greek alphabet around 720–700BC. . . . The new way to store knowledge was not in mnemonic formulas but in the written text" (p. 24). What happened in writing "freed the mind for more original, more abstract thought. . . . Plato excluded from his ideal republic poets," because "he found himself in a new chirographically styled noetic world in which the formula or cliche, beloved of all traditional poets, was outmoded and counterproductive" (p. 24). From this idea it becomes clear that, intellectually, literacy is preferred over orality. There has been an ongoing debate regarding the primacy of speech over writing among academicians in the past twenty years or so.

Chapter II

1. These lonely houses that have fallen into ruin are reminiscent of a house in a lovely sonnet by Frederick Goddard Tuckerman (1931), sonnet 16 of the second series, which I would like to quote here in its entirety.

> Under the mountain, as when first I knew
> Its low dark roof and chimney creeper-twined,
> The red house stands; and yet my footsteps find,
> Vague in the walks, waste balm and feverfew.
> But they are gone: no soft-eyed sisters trip
> Across the porch or lintels; where, behind,
> The mother sat, sat knitting with pursed lip.
> The house stands vacant in its green recess,
> Absent of beauty as a broken heart.
> The wild rain enters, and the sunset wind
> Sighs in the chambers of their loveliness
> Or shakes the pane—and in the silent noons
> The glass falls from the window, part by part,
> And ringeth faintly in the grassy stones.

Chapter III

1. It might be argued that realism is not so much a means for shoring up fantasy as it is the means by which fantasy opens up new possibilities in real life.

2. There were four Tenadooah brothers. The two oldest brothers were Tainpeah and Daugomah. Their names became the surnames of all their offspring. Unless people know the naming process followed in the late nineteenth century, they will not realize that some Kiowa families are members of the nuclear family even though their last names indicate otherwise.

3. It was always difficult to resume conversation after a hiatus. It could take hours to reestablish rapport with my storytelling consultants, and at first I found the process very unnerving. I was always afraid I would have to start the interview all over again. Generally, I would begin an interview by reminding my coworkers that I thought we could pick up our talk from where we had left off. But my consultants did not always remember what we had talked about, much less when. Luckily, I had kept good notes and had tape recordings, so that I had simply to reengage my consultants, gradually working back to the last stopping place.

Notes

Chapter IV

1. *The Dialogic Imagination*, M. M. Bakhtin, edited by Michael Holquist (1981), set some new standards in the criticism of novels and storytelling. Many scholars of American Indian literature use Bakhtin as a standard source in their work.

Chapter V

1. Óhòmàu is the sacred war dance society of the Kiowas. Given to Kiowas long ago by the Omaha tribe as a token of friendship in the form of a sacred dance bustle, songs, and dance, the society holds a powwow every year at the Óhòmàu ceremonial grounds west of Anadarko, Oklahoma. Only Kiowa males may become members of the dance society.

2. Father Isadore Ricklin (1890s?), a Benedictine priest at St. Patrick's Mission, Anadarko, Oklahoma, purportedly attended peyote meetings conducted by Kiowas. One of the first priests assigned to Indian territory in this part of the country, Isadore was a good man, my grandfather said. When I asked him if the old priest ate peyote, he said he did just like any other peyote celebrant. "He had big whiskers," my grandfather said. "We called him Sénpàuzélbé [Terrible Whiskers] for that reason."

Later, there were other priests who frequented those nocturnal prayer meetings. Father Edward Bock, another Benedictine assigned to St. Patrick's from 1959 until the mid-1960s, thought peyote a fine spiritual sacrament, just as the Indians who still use it do. They generally oppose the view that it is a substance. Today only members of the chartered Native American Church may legally purchase peyote, religious use guaranteed by the Freedom of Religion Act of 1988. Father Bock found much Christian or Catholic symbolism in the peyote ritual. He pointed out some obvious symbols in the cross, the burning of incense, the blessing over the water, and the peyote staff, which is an instrument held in the hand of the peyote singer as he sings.

3. In the true spirit of the peyote religion, a person who is a practitioner has a personal attachment to it through a family or "father" (his father, grandfather, or some other close relative) who owned and conducted the peyote meeting. Special peyote is placed in the center of the moon altar as a symbol of the unity and spirit of the meeting, and it remains there throughout the ceremony. Without this sacred symbol it is virtually impossible to conduct a meeting.

4. "Dialogue," contends Greg Sarris (1993), "in the most general sense is understood as conversation between two or more people, people talking back and forth

with one another. M. M. Bakhtin sees dialogue as an essential characteristic of the novel, which, for Bakhtin, is comprised of a diversity of voices. Heteroglossia is Bakhtin's term, or major trope, for the multitude of voices that comprise not only the novel but all other forms and elements of communication" (p. 4).

5. Parker McKenzie's father, General McKenzie, was a Kiowa captive. Parker told me he was taken as a boy by the Mescalero Apaches somewhere in New Mexico. Later, he was traded to the Comanches before coming to the Kiowas. Kiowas took many Mexican and white captives on the southern Plains (Mooney 1898), perhaps more than any other tribe. Oscar's remark about Parker's ethnicity should not be taken as disparaging but as ironic humor. Outsiders do not always catch the Kiowa humor and teasing that goes on among Kiowa relatives and acquaintances and may misunderstand. Many Kiowas are in fact descendants of Mexican and white captives.

Tháukáuimá (White Woman), my grandfather's maternal grandmother, was either a Spanish or Mexican captive. The joke in our family was that no matter how much we teased other Kiowas about their diluted bloodlines we were ourselves descendants of non-Kiowas.

6. That chuckling is sometimes a hindrance to beginning speakers was explained to me by a young Kiowa woman who recently remarked at a Kiowa language class in Anadarko: "They laugh at you. I try to say it right but I can't. I don't mind speaking. But I'm afraid I'll say it wrong. I never tried because I thought I was going to be wrong. My grandma tried to help me say things but I just couldn't do it. I guess I need practice."

Chapter VI

1. There is a famous story Parker McKenzie tells about a butchering event near Gotebo, Oklahoma, which I do not include here. That story quickly became popular when I was working at the Kiowa Elders Center in the 1980s. Cornelius recorded it and made sure I heard it some twelve years later. He made a few remarks about the story and added some comical anecdotes of his own, and in doing so created a storytelling event with tribal framing and social context.

2. There are apparently a number of bót stories in the Kiowa oral canon of comical stories. Perhaps they are a part of a separate genre of personal narratives with a mixture of fiction and joking. The point of the narratives is to make somebody look foolish or be the butt end of the joke. Kiowas, it would appear, love eating bót but are at the same time slightly ashamed, and this conflict is what accounts for these stories.

Notes

3. The name is a one-sentence word, an example of what linguists call incorporation. Kiowas are often given names that are stories or events in and of themselves. In time the name is abbreviated. For example, Yí:sàum is the short or abbreviated version of the name of someone who went into battle and emerged unscathed twice and his fellow warriors saw him and therefore gave him that name to memorialize the event and his bravery. It is the name given to Parker McKenzie.

4. See Basso (1979), a good study of Western Apache Indian humor and storytelling.

Chapter VII

1. For more, see J. J. Methvin (1996).

2. Blackleggings was a Kiowa warrior society. The young men in the story were performing a ceremonial blackleggings dance.

Chapter VIII

1. There were apparently rivalries among Kiowa medicine men, who competed and tried to outdo one another. They often put spells or curses on each other to demonstrate how powerful they were. The man with the strongest *dáui* (medicine) proved his worth among his peers and was held in high esteem. One of the most powerful Kiowa medicine men in the nineteenth century was Snapping Turtle, who became a major figure in Kiowa folklore.

Works Cited

Addonizio, Kim, and Dorianne Laux. (1997) *The Poet's Companion*. New York: W. W. Norton & Co.

Aristotle. (1954) *Rhetoric and Poetics*. Translated by W. Rhys Roberts and Ingram Bywater. New York: Modern Library.

Bachelard, Gaston. (1971) *On Poetic Imagination and Reverie*. Translated by Colette Gaudin. Indianapolis: Bobbs-Merrill.

Bakhtin, M. M. (1981) *The Dialogic Imagination*. Edited by Michael Holquist. Austin: University of Texas Press.

Bascom, William (1965) The Forms of Folklore: Prose Narratives. *Journal of American Folklore* 78:3–20.

Basso, Keith. (1990) *Western Apache Language and Culture: Essays in Linguistic Anthropology*. Tucson: University of Arizona Press.

———. (1979) *Portraits of the Whiteman*. Cambridge: Cambridge University Press.

Basso, Keith, and Steven Feld, eds. (1996) *Senses of Place*. Santa Fe, N.M.: School of American Research Press.

Bauman, Richard. (1977) *Verbal Art as Performance*. Prospect Heights, Ill.: Waveland Press.

———. (1986) *Story, Performance and Event: Contextual Studies of Oral Narrative*. Cambridge: Cambridge University Press.

Bauman, Richard, and Charles L. Briggs. (1990) Poetics and Performance as Critical Perspectives on Language and Social Life. *Annual Review of Anthropology* 19:59–88.

Becker, A. (1995) *Beyond Translation: Essays toward a Modern Philology*. Ann Arbor: University of Michigan Press.

Blaeser, Kimberly. (1970) The Existing Body of American Indian Writing and Voids

That Need Filling. A talk at the American Indian Voices: A Regional Literary Symposium. The Wisconsin Academy of Sciences, Arts and Letters. Racine, Wis.

Bourdieu, Pierre (1990) *Outline of a Theory of Practice*. Translated by Richard Nice. Cambridge: Cambridge University Press.

Boyd, Maurice. (1981) *Kiowa Voices: Ceremonial Dance, Ritual and Song*. Vol. 1. Fort Worth: Texas Christian University Press.

———. (1983) *Kiowa Voices: Myths, Legends and Folktales*. Vol. 2. Fort Worth: Texas Christian University Press.

Clifford, James. (1983) On Ethnographic Authority. *Representations* 1, 2:118–46.

Deacon, Desley. (1997) *Elsie Clews Parsons: Inventing Modern Life*. Chicago: University of Chicago Press.

Deloria, Vine, Jr. (1969) *Custer Died for Your Sins*. New York: Avon Books.

Dorian, N. (1981) *Language Death: The Life Cycle of a Scottish Gaelic Dialect*. Philadelphia: University of Pennsylvania Press.

Duranti, A., and C. Goodwin, eds. (1992) *Rethinking Context: Language as Interactive Phenomenon*. Cambridge: Cambridge University Press.

Fasold, R. (1984) *The Sociolinguistics of Society*. Oxford: Basil Blackwell.

Finnegan, Ruth. (1977) *Oral Poetry*. Cambridge: Cambridge University Press.

Foley, John M., ed. (1990) *Oral-Formulaic Theory*. New York: Garland Publishing, Inc.

Foley, William A. (1997) *Anthropological Linguistics*. Malden, Mass., and Oxford: Blackwell Publishers Ltd.

Gal, S. (1979) *Language Shift: Social Determinants of Linguistic Change in Bilingual Austria*. New York: Academic Press.

Geertz, Clifford. (1973) *The Interpretation of Cultures*. New York: Basic Books.

Goffman, Erving. (1974) *Frame Analysis*. New York: Harper & Row.

Gumperz, J. (1982) *Discourse Strategies*. Cambridge: Cambridge University Press.

Harrington, John P. (1928) *Vocabulary of the Kiowa Language*. Bureau of American Ethnology Bulletin 84. Washington, D.C: Government Printing Office.

Havelock, Eric A. (1963) *Preface to Plato*. Cambridge: Belknap Press of Harvard University Press.

Hewett, Edgar L., and Bertha P. Dutton. (1945) *The Pueblo Indian World*. Albuquerque: University of New Mexico and the School of American Research.

Hyde, Lewis. (1983) *The Gift: Imagination on the Erotic Life of Property*. New York: Random House.

Hymes, Dell. (1977) Discovering Oral Performance and Measured Verse in American Indian Narrative. *New Literary History* 8:431–57.

Works Cited

———. (1981) *In Vain I Tried to Tell You: Essays in Native American Ethnopoetics*. Philadelphia: University of Pennsylvania Press.

Jaynes, Julian. (1976) *The Origin of Consciousness in the Breakdown of the Bicameral Mind*. Boston: Houghton Mifflin Co.

Kracht, Benjamin. (1997) Kiowa Religion in Historical Perspective. *American Indian Quarterly* 21:15–33.

Kulick, D. (1992) *Language Shift and Cultural Reproduction*. Cambridge: Cambridge University Press.

Lassiter, Eric. (2000) Commentary: Authoritative Texts, Collaborative Ethnography, and Native American Studies. *American Indian Quarterly* 24:601–14.

Lawless, Elaine. (1992) "I Was Afraid Someone Like You . . . An Outsider . . . Would Misunderstand": Negotiating Interpretive Difference between Ethnographers and Subjects. *Journal of American Folklore* 105:301–14.

Lord, Albert B. (1960) *The Singer of Tales*. Harvard Studies in Comparative Literature, 24. Cambridge,: Harvard University Press.

Malinowski, Bronislaw. (1922) The Essentials of the Kula. *Anthropological Theory*. Mountain View, Calif.: Mayfield Publishing Co.

Marriott, Alice. (1945) *The Ten Grandmothers*. Norman: University of Oklahoma Press.

———. (1947) *Winter-telling Stories*. New York: Thomas Y. Crowell.

———. (1963) *Saynday's People*. Lincoln: University of Nebraska Press.

Mauss, Marcel. (1990 [1925]) *The Gift: The Form and Reason for Exchange in Archaic Societies*. Translated by W. D. Halls. New York: W. W. Norton Co.

McGee, Jon R., and Richard L. Warms. (1996) The Gift, by Marcel Mauss. *Anthropological Theory*. Mountain View, Calif.: Mayfield Publishing Co.

McKenzie, Parker P. (n.d.) The Essential Elements of the Kiowa Language. Unpublished ms. Mountain View, Okla.

———. (n.d.) Notes and Correspondences. Mountain View, Okla.

McLuhan, Marshall. (1962) *The Gutenberg Galaxy: The Making of Typographic Man*. Toronto: University of Toronto Press.

Meadows, William C. (1999) *Kiowa, Apache, and Comanche Military Societies*. Austin: University of Texas Press.

Methvin, J. J. (1996) *Andele: The Mexican-Kiowa Captive*. Albuquerque: University of New Mexico Press.

Momaday, N. Scott. (1968) *House Made of Dawn*. New Yorker: Harper.

———. (1969) *The Way to Rainy Mountain*. Albuquerque: University of New Mexico Press.

———. (1970) The Man Made of Words. Speech at the First Convocation of American Indian Scholars, Dartmouth College, Hanover, N.H.

Mooney, James. (1898) *Calendar History of the Kiowa Indians*. Seventeenth Annual Report of the Bureau of American Ethnology. Washington, D.C.: Smithsonian Institution Press.

Nye, S. W. (1962) *Bad Medicine and Good*. Norman: University of Oklahoma Press.

Okpewho, Isidore. (1979) *The Epic in Africa: Toward a Poetics of the Oral Performance*. New York: Columbia University Press.

Ong, Walter J. (1982) *Orality and Literacy*. London: Routledge.

Parry, Adam, ed. (1971) Introduction, and notes, *The Making of Homeric Verse: The Collected Papers of Milman Parry*. Oxford: Clarendon Press.

Parsons, Elsie C. (1929) *Kiowa Tales*. New York: American Folklore Society, G. E. Stechert and Co.

Radin, Paul. (1969) *The Trickster: A Study in American Indian Mythology*. New York: Greenwood Press.

Ricoeur, Paul. (1981) *Hermeneutics and the Human Sciences*. Edited by John B. Thompson. New York: Cambridge University Press.

Rosen, Leo. (1982) *Hooray For Yiddish*. New York: Simon and Schuster.

Sapir, E. (1921) *Language: An Introduction to the Study of Speech*. New York: Harcourt, Brace and World.

Sarris, Greg. (1989) The Last Woman from Cache Creek: Conversations with Mabel McKay. Ph.D. dissertation. Stanford University.

———. (1993) *Keeping Slug Woman Alive*. Berkeley: University Of California Press.

Saussure, F. (1959 [1916]) *Course in General Linguistics*. New York: McGraw-Hill.

Tedlock, Barbara. (1991) From Participant Observation to the Observation of Participation: The Emergence of Narrative Ethnography. *Journal of Anthropological Research* 47:69–94.

Tedlock, Dennis. (1983) *The Spoken Word and the Work of Interpretation*. Philadelphia: University of Pennsylvania Press.

Tuckerman, Frederick G. (1931) *The Sonnets of Frederick Goddard Tuckerman*. New York: A. A. Knopf.

Turner, Victor. (1967) Betwixt and Between: the Liminal Period in Rites of Passage. *The Forest of Symbols: Aspects of Ndembu Ritual*. Ithaca: Cornell University Press.

Watkins, Laurel J. (1984) *A Grammar of Kiowa*. Lincoln: University of Nebraska Press.

Whorf, Benjamin. (1956) *Language, Thought, and Reality: Selected Writings of Benjamin Lee Whorf*. Cambridge: MIT Press.

Index

Index

Index

60; on magic realism, 13–14; on performative frame and mode, 59; on storytelling responses, 68–69; on verisimilitude, 13; on Zuni storytelling, 13–14, 34, 130–31n. 5, 131n. 7

Tenadooah (old man), 52, 55, 116–17

Ten Grandmothers. *See* Tàlídàui

themes, story. *See* characters and themes

Tofpi, John, xi, xvi; in dialogic exchange, 42, 45, 111–13; at Slick Hills, 17–19; on storytelling questions, 6; telling the dream story, 14–15, 20–29, 31–32

tornado. *See* Storm Spirit

trade, kula, xix

traditions, Kiowa, 93

tribalism, xviii

Trobriand people, xix

Tsoodle, Oscar, 10–11, 56, 92; making old texts into new texts, 92–103; narrating "The Mother Deer, Her Death Song," 52–54; telling stories within stories, 63–79

Turner, Victor: on context of action, xxii; on symbolic activities, xxii; on symbolic objects, xxii; on symbols and social processes, xxi

Udder-Angry-Ones, 3

Uncle Oscar. *See* Tsoodle, Oscar

values, Kiowa, xiv

vowels, xxix

Watkins, Laurel J., xxv

Western History Collection (University of Oklahoma), 80

Western literature, classical, xxiii

Wevoka, 90

Willis, Carole, 104–10

yellow paint (gùtqógùl:àum:gà), 17

Yellowstone, 3

Yí:sàum. *See* McKenzie, Parker, P.

Zuni, 13, 34, 79; narratives, 130n. 5; poetics, 131n. 7; social organization, 130n. 5; story, 131n. 7; story at Corn Mountain, 130n. 5. *See also* Tedlock, Dennis

Zuni storytellers. *See* Peynetsa, Andrew; Peynetsa, Joseph; Tedlock, Dennis

About the Author

Over the years, Gus Palmer Jr. has written poetry, fiction, and essays and translated Kiowa stories into English. Crediting his grandfather and the late Kiowa linguist Parker McKenzie for all the Kiowa he knows, he is currently at work on a book of Kiowa traditional stories that will be transcribed in Kiowa and translated into English. Because of the rapid decline in Kiowa speakers, it is important to document as many oral narratives as possible, Palmer says. But his main interest is and has for a long time been the revitalization and preservation of Kiowa, spoken Kiowa.

He attended the University of Oklahoma, where he is now an assistant professor in the anthropology department. He has published poetry in a number of anthologies and magazines and also wrote and directed a motion picture that won film awards. Concentrating mainly on linguistic anthropology and American Indian languages and literatures, he still writes stories and poetry when the occasion presents itself. He has been experimenting with writing poems in Kiowa. "Like Italian and, to some extent, Spanish," he says, "Kiowa has word endings that work nicely into sound patterns for use in poems."